# *A Handbook for* CHURCHWARDENS AND PAROCHIAL CHURCH COUNCILLORS

BY

## KENNETH M. MACMORRAN
M.A., LL.B.
*One of Her Majesty's Counsel*
*Formerly Chancellor of the Dioceses*
*of Chichester, Lincoln, Ely, St Albans, Newcastle and Guildford*

and

## KENNETH J. T. ELPHINSTONE
M.A.
*Barrister-at-Law, and Clerk in Holy Orders,*
*Chancellor of the Dioceses of York, Chester and Hereford*

MOWBRAYS
LONDON & OXFORD

© *A. R. Mowbray & Company Ltd 1971*

*Printed in Great Britain by*
*Alden & Mowbray Ltd at the Alden Press, Oxford*

SBN 264 65140 5

*First published in November, 1921*
*New Edition, 1957*
*Twenty-ninth impression, revised, 1959*
*Thirtieth impression, 1961*
*New edition, 1966*
*New edition, 1971*

## INTRODUCTION

The first edition of this book was published nearly fifty years ago in November 1921. Since then, in successive editions, there have been relatively minor alterations in the light of the various changes in the law which have been made from time to time. These apart, the original text has been kept more or less intact.

In the case of this present edition, more radical alterations have been necessary. The Pastoral Measure 1968 and the Synodical Government Measure 1969 have so revolutionised the system of Church government and administration, from the parochial level upwards, that much of the book has had to be completely re-written. And those two Measures form only a part (even if the most important part) of the large body of legislation passed during the last ten years or so which affects the subject-matter of the book.

Through all its editions, the book has had two objects: first, to provide useful information about the functions of church-wardens and parochial church councillors, as far as possible in untechnical language; and secondly, to set this information in the context of the general system of Church government, so that the office-holder in the parish may be given an idea of his place within the organisation of the Church of England as a whole. The authors of this edition have had these two objects always in mind. At the same time, they have endeavoured to keep the size of the book within such a compass that the use of the word 'Handbook' in its title may still be justified.

# CONTENTS

v

# A Handbook for Churchwardens and Parochial Church Councillors

# CHAPTER I

## THE CONSTITUTION OF THE CHURCH

(1) The Province — (2) The Diocese — (3) The Archdeaconry — (4) The Rural Deanery.

### (1) THE PROVINCE

The Province of Canterbury, consisting of twenty-nine, and the Province of York, consisting of fourteen, dioceses, together constitute the Church of England as far as this country is concerned. With the other Churches in communion with the See of Canterbury and the overseas provinces this work is not concerned. Each of the Provinces of Canterbury and York is under the direction of an archbishop, and both the archbishops preside over dioceses as well as exercising their archi-episcopal authority in their respective provinces.

An archbishop is president of his convocation and he issues his mandate for the assembly of that body on receipt of a writ from the Crown. During a vacancy in the see of a diocese within the province he provides for the ecclesiastical administration of that diocese in his capacity of 'guardian of the spiritualities'[1] for the whole province. He normally nominates a suffragan or assistant bishop for the purpose. It is his duty to consecrate new bishops, including suffragan bishops, although his participation in the consecration is not necessary to its validity. A bishop holding office within the province swears an oath of canonical obedience to the archbishop.

The Archbishops of Canterbury and York have the special styles respectively of Primate of All England and Metropolitan, and Primate of England and Metropolitan. Both of them are always members of the House of Lords.

[1] A vacant arch-see is administered by the dean and the chapter.

1

## (2) THE DIOCESE

The diocese is a defined territory presided over by a bishop, who has an exclusive jurisdiction within it. In some statutes and in the Prayer Book, the bishop is spoken of as the 'Ordinary', i.e. as having ordinary jurisdiction in ecclesiastical matters within his diocese. This denotes as resident in the diocesan an original as distinct from a delegated jurisdiction.

The principle which underlies the whole system of the spiritual government of the Church is that of vesting the government of each diocese in the bishop of that diocese. This dominant idea is to be seen in actual working every day. Thus no bishop may presume to exercise any episcopal function in the diocese of another without the consent of the diocesan, and he may be inhibited from so doing. Again, the diocesan bishop institutes an incumbent to his cure, and that incumbent has no rights in his parish until the institution has taken place. Nor has an assistant curate any rights in his office until he has been licensed by the bishop. Nor can a layman take upon himself the office of reader without the bishop's permission.

At the same time, the Anglican episcopate is a constitutional episcopate and not an absolutely monarchical one. In this respect the bishop is bound in several ways. He is the centre and head of his diocese, and the unity of the Church requires that this should be so. But at his consecration he takes an oath of obedience to the archbishop, and he is bound to govern his diocese in accordance with the law of the Church. Under the Synodical Government Measure 1969, the duty is expressly imposed on him to consult with the diocesan synod[1] on matters of general concern and importance to the diocese.

It is, perhaps, hardly necessary to add that in ruling his diocese, a bishop must conform to the secular law so far as it is applicable. His duties are regulated in innumerable matters by common law and statute, and so far as these are of intimate concern to the laity, mention is made of them in their appropriate context in the chapters which follow.

In addition to the two archbishops, the Bishops of London, Durham and Winchester, together with twenty-one other dio-

[1] See p. 12 *post*.

cesan bishops according to seniority of appointment as diocesans, have seats in the House of Lords.

Dioceses are divided into archdeaconries, which in turn consist of rural deaneries. These units are interposed between the parish and the diocese for certain purposes, although the two latter are the only units necessary to a parochial system. It follows that as a general rule each parish is in (1) a rural deanery, (2) an archdeaconry, (3) a diocese, and (4) a province. The two latter have been briefly described.

## (3) THE ARCHDEACONRY

An archdeaconry may extend to the whole of a diocese, but is usually smaller. At its head is the archdeacon, who on appointment must have completed at least six years in priest's orders. He is usually (though not always) appointed by the bishop, and before entering upon his office subscribes the declaration of assent to the Articles of Religion and the Prayer Book, the declaration against simony, and the oath of allegiance. An archdeacon is entitled by custom to the style of address 'The Venerable'.

Subject to the paramount rights of the bishop of the diocese, an archdeacon has the power of visitation within his archdeaconry, and it is at his visitation after the end of April (when the bishop does not hold one) that churchwardens are admitted to office. This visitation is the only remaining vestige of the archdeacon's court. It is important to remember that it is a judicial proceeding, because the archdeacon has to be satisfied that the persons chosen as churchwardens are fit and proper for the office, after hearing (if necessary) any objections which may be presented to him.

In addition, powers are conferred on the archdeacon for the enforcement of the provisions for the quinquennial inspection of churches contained in the Inspection of Churches Measure 1955. He also 'inducts' clergy who are presented to benefices, i.e. places them in possession of the *temporalities* of the benefice.

The archdeacon is a member of the Diocesan Board of Patronage when that Board is transacting any business relating to a benefice in his archdeaconry.

One of the archdeacons in every diocese is a member of the

Lower House of Convocation, and of the House of Clergy of the General Synod.

## (4) THE RURAL DEANERY

The rural deanery is a collection of parishes for administrative purposes within an archdeaconry. Its significance as an ecclesiastical unit has recently been enhanced as a result of the creation, by the Synodical Government Measure 1969, of deanery synods, in which important functions are vested.[1]

Each rural deanery is presided over by a rural dean who is usually (though not necessarily) one of the beneficed clergy in the deanery. He is the bishop's officer and may be removed from office at any time.

Under the Synodical Government Measure 1969, he receives notice of appeal against the allowance or disallowance of enrolment on the electoral roll, or of a vote, or against the result of any election at parochial or deanery level. Apart from this and a few other statutory functions, his duties are such (e.g. of inquiry and report about specific matters) as may from time to time be deputed to him by the bishop or archdeacon. According to some authorities he may, in the absence of the archdeacon, 'induct' to a benefice; but it is doubtful whether he is qualified to do this except as the archdeacon's deputy.

The rural dean is a member of the Diocesan Board of Patronage when that Board is transacting any business relating to a benefice in his deanery. He, and an elected member of the house of laity of the deanery synod, are joint chairmen of that synod.

[1] See p. 16 *post*.

# SYNODICAL GOVERNMENT

## (1) PRELIMINARY NOTE

Down to the year 1919, the Sovereign in Parliament was the only institution having unlimited power to legislate for the affairs of the Church of England. An Act of Parliament could (as it still can) effect any alteration whatever in the law of the Church.

A subsidiary legislative power was vested in the two Convocations of Canterbury and York, which, after a long lapse, had been revived in 1852 and 1861 respectively. The Convocation of each province consisted of two Houses; an Upper House composed of the diocesan bishops of the province under the presidency of the archbishop; and a Lower House of inferior clergy, composed in part of *ex-officio* members (deans, archdeacons and others), and in part of proctors (i.e. elected representatives) for cathedral chapters and for the beneficed clergy.

Each Convocation had power to legislate by passing canons, but it was a strictly conditional and limited power. In the first place, a canon, to be effective at all, required the royal assent; secondly, it was only effective within the province whose Convocation passed it; thirdly, it was ineffective in so far as it conflicted with existing common law or statute; and finally, a canon was directly binding only on the clergy, and not on the laity.

In the early years of the twentieth century there was a strong and growing feeling that the Church should have more independence in the management of its affairs, and in particular that the laity of the Church should be given a larger voice in such management. The movement to that end eventually bore fruit in the passage through Parliament of the Church of England Assembly (Powers) Act 1919. This Act established the body called 'The National Assembly of the Church of England' ('The Church

5

Assembly' for short), in which was vested a general power, subject to the control of Parliament, to legislate as to matters concerning the Church of England.

Stated very shortly, the general scheme of the Act was as follows. The Church Assembly, as constituted by the Act, consisted of three Houses: the House of Bishops, the House of Clergy, and the House of Laity. Power was conferred on the Assembly to propose and pass new laws called 'Measures'. Any measure, having been passed in the Assembly by a majority of the members of each House present and voting, and having been (in effect) endorsed by resolution of both Houses of Parliament, and having received the royal assent, was given the same force and effect as an Act of Parliament.

In passing this Act, Parliament did not deprive itself of its own power of legislating for the Church; but in practice, since the Act came into force, it has rarely if ever done so, except in relation to private or local matters, or in cases in which, for any reason, a measure of the Church Assembly might have been deemed inappropriate.

The power of the Convocations to make canons was not affected by the Act. This power was in fact exercised, in 1964 and 1969, by the production of a comprehensive new set of canons for the Church of England as a whole.[1] The new canons superseded (with relatively minor exceptions) the previous code of canons issued in 1603 (much of which had become obsolete) and certain other canons which had been subsequently made from time to time.

The principle of lay participation at all levels was implemented by the setting up of diocesan conferences and (in most though not all dioceses) of ruri-decanal conferences, both of which bodies had a mixed clerical and lay membership; and by the establishment in the parishes of parochial church councils, consisting in the main of elected representatives of the laity.

Diocesan and ruri-decanal conferences have been rendered obsolete by the Synodical Government Measure 1969, and it is, therefore, unnecessary to consider their composition and func-

[1] Each of the new canons was passed in identical form by both Convocations. As a matter of grace (not of legal necessity) the approval of the House of Laity of the Church Assembly was obtained to each canon before it was actually passed.

tions, save only to mention that it fell to the lay members of the diocesan conference to elect representatives from the diocese to the House of Laity of the Church Assembly.

Parochial church councils are the subject-matter of a later chapter in this book.

## (2) SCHEME OF SYNODICAL GOVERNMENT

The Synodical Government Measure 1969, whilst building on the scheme of Church government established in 1919 and subsequent years, has introduced such considerable alterations and reforms that it creates, in effect, a more or less entirely new system.

The objects of the Measure are two-fold:

(a) To provide a sound organisation at every level of Church government, and better communications from the top downwards and *vice versa*, so as to ensure an easy flow of information and ideas in both directions; and

(b) to give the laity a larger say in the government of the Church at all levels, and in particular in relation to the doctrines and services of the Church.

Under the scheme introduced by the Measure, 'synods', each of them with a mixed clerical and lay membership, are established at the national, diocesan and ruri-decanal levels; such synods being known as the 'General Synod', 'diocesan synods' and 'deanery synods' respectively. The General Synod is continuous in identity with the former Church Assembly, but it has been largely re-constituted, and it inherits not only the power of the Church Assembly to legislate by measure, but also the former power of the Convocations to make canons (which power has been transferred to it from the Convocations). The diocesan and deanery synods are newly created bodies, although they correspond roughly with the former diocesan and ruri-decanal conferences.

The composition and functions of each of the synods which have been referred to are briefly stated later on in this chapter.

## (3) CONVOCATIONS

But first it is necessary to make some further mention of the Convocations. These bodies, although the power of making canons has been taken away from them, still maintain a separate existence for certain purposes.

Each Convocation still consists, as before, of an Upper House of diocesan bishops, and a Lower House of inferior clergy (though it now has power to add to itself by standing order a third House, viz. a House of Laity, for such of its functions as it may determine).

As part of the scheme of synodical government, the Lower House of each Convocation has been considerably reduced from its former size. The Lower House of the Province of Canterbury now has a maximum membership of 176, made up as follows:

(1) Ten of their own number elected by the deans and provosts of cathedrals, and the deans of Westminster Abbey and St. George's Chapel, Windsor;
(2) Either the Dean of Jersey or the Dean of Guernsey;
(3) One archdeacon from each diocese;
(4) The three Chaplains to the Forces;
(5) One representative of the ordained members of religious communities in the Province;
(6) Four proctors for the universities;
(7) Proctors for the diocesan clergy not exceeding 126;
(8) Not more than two co-opted members.

The proctors for diocesan clergy are elected in the manner following:

(i) The electoral area is the diocese.
(ii) The total number of proctors is apportioned between the dioceses according to the number of electors in each diocese.
(iii) Generally speaking, the electors include suffragan and assistant bishops, together with clergymen beneficed in the diocese, or licensed under seal by the bishop, or holding office in a cathedral, or in Westminster Abbey or St. George's Chapel, Windsor. But deans, provosts, archdeacons and members of religious communities are not entitled to vote, and no-one is entitled to vote in more than one diocese.
(iv) All persons in priest's orders who are entitled to vote are eligible for election, and so is an archdeacon who is not otherwise a member of the Lower House.

In the Province of York, the maximum membership is eighty-two, made up of five representative deans or provosts, one archdeacon from each diocese, one representative of religious communities, two university proctors, not more than sixty-one diocesan proctors, and not more than one co-opted member. The rules as to the election of diocesan proctors are the same as for Canterbury.

The Convocations are called together and dissolved in pursuance of the Royal Writ. Until the passing of the Church of England Convocations Act 1966, their life was linked to that of Parliament, so that when Parliament was dissolved they also stood dissolved; by virtue of the Act this has ceased to be so. But although the existence of the Convocations is now independent of that of Parliament, their life, like the life of Parliament, is limited to a maximum of five years.

## (4) GENERAL SYNOD (COMPOSITION)

The General Synod, being the same body as the former Church Assembly under another name, consists of the same three Houses.

The House of Bishops is composed of the combined membership of the Upper Houses of the two Convocations (i.e. of all the diocesan bishops of both Provinces).

The House of Clergy is composed of the combined membership of the Lower Houses of the two Convocations. As a result of the recent reduction in the membership of the Lower Houses, the membership of the House of Clergy has been reduced from a former 347 to a maximum of 258.

The House of Laity has likewise been reduced in number. Before the Synodical Government Measure 1969 came into force, it had 347 members. Under the Measure, the maximum is now 263, made up as follows:

(1) Not more than 250 members elected from the dioceses;
(2) Two representatives of the lay members of religious communities;
(3) A maximum of six *ex-officio* members, being six ecclesiastical officials specified in the Measure, provided they are not in holy orders;
(4) Not more than five co-opted members.

The rules as to the election of members from the dioceses are briefly as follows:

B

(i) The electoral area is the diocese, subject to a power for a diocesan synod to divide its diocese into two or more areas, and to apportion the number of members to be elected for the diocese among such areas.

(ii) The total number of members to be elected (fixed, subject to the maximum of 250, by resolution of the General Synod) is apportioned, in the first place, between the Provinces of Canterbury and York as nearly as possible in the proportion of sixty-eight to thirty-two; and in the second place between the dioceses within each province, according to the total number of names on the electoral rolls[1] of all the parishes of each diocese.

(iii) The electors in each diocese are the members of the houses of laity of all the deanery synods in the diocese, other than co-opted members.

(iv) Any lay person is eligible for election who is an 'actual communicant member'[2] of the Church of England of age to vote at a Parliamentary election, and whose name is entered on the roll of any parish in the diocese, or who is a habitual worshipper at any cathedral church in the diocese.[3]

The General Synod must meet at least twice a year. Its joint Presidents are the two Archbishops, one of whom, or one of an appointed panel of chairmen, is chairman at any meeting of the Synod as a whole.

The life of a General Synod is co-terminous with that of the Convocations. There is provision whereby, on a dissolution of the General Synod, any boards, commissions, committees or other bodies of the dissolved Synod may continue their proceedings during the period of dissolution, and members of the dissolved Synod may continue to act thereon.

## (5) GENERAL SYNOD (FUNCTIONS)

The functions of the General Synod, as laid down by the Measure (Schedule 2, paragraph 6), are as follows:

'(a) to consider matters concerning the Church of England and to make provision in respect thereof—

[1] As to electoral rolls see p. 76 *post*.

[2] For the definition of this expression see p. 102 *post*.

[3] Including Westminster Abbey and St. George's Chapel, Windsor, in the appropriate dioceses.

(i) by measure intended to be given, in the manner prescribed by the Church of England Assembly (Powers) Act 1919, the force and effect of an Act of Parliament, or

(ii) by Canon made, promulged and executed in accordance with the like provisions and subject to the like restrictions and having the like legislative force as Canons heretofore made, promulged and executed by the Convocations of Canterbury and York, or

(iii) by such order, regulation or other subordinate instrument as may be authorised by Measure or Canon, or

(iv) by such Act of Synod, regulation or other instrument or proceeding as may be appropriate in cases where provision by or under a Measure or Canon is not required;

(b) to consider and express their opinion on any other matters of religious or public interest.'

The function of making canons is exercisable by the General Synod for the Church of England as a whole instead of being exercisable provincially (as in the case of canons formerly made by one or other of the Convocations); but this is without prejudice to the making of different provisions, where appropriate, for the two provinces.

A motion for the final approval of a measure or canon requires the assent of the majority of the members of each House present and voting. Other motions (subject to a qualification affecting procedural motions) are determined by a majority of the members of the whole Synod present and voting.

Provisions which concern doctrinal formulae, or the services or ceremonies of the Church, or the administration of sacraments or sacred rites, are subject to special safeguards. Any such provision can only be submitted for final approval by the Synod in a form which has been previously proposed by the House of Bishops. And if either of the Convocations, or the House of Laity, so require, it cannot be submitted for final approval by the Synod unless it has previously been approved by each House of both Convocations and by the House of Laity.

Any measure providing for permanent changes in the Services of Baptism or Holy Communion or in the Ordinal, or any scheme for a constitutional union or a permanent and substantial change of relationship between the Church of England and another Christian body, is not to be finally approved by the Synod unless it has been previously approved in substance by a majority of the dioceses at meetings of their diocesan synods.

The procedure for passing measures of the General Synod into law involves an inter-relationship between two committees, viz. a 'Legislative Committee' which is a committee of the General Synod appointed from all three of its Houses; and an 'Ecclesiastical Committee' which is a joint committee of both Houses of Parliament.

The procedure in question may be summarised as follows. The General Synod passes a resolution that legislation by measure on some matter concerning the Church is desirable. Probably such a resolution will be passed in consequence of a report which has been presented to, and adopted by, the Synod. A 'measure' is then drafted to give effect to the resolution, which measure is discussed and passed (with or without modification) by the Synod. It is then referred to the Legislative Committee, which considers it and may make comments or explanations thereon. It then forwards the measure to the Ecclesiastical Committee, which drafts a report on the measure stating its nature and legal effect, and containing the views of the Committee on its expediency and its relation to the constitutional rights of all Her Majesty's subjects. This draft report before being presented to Parliament must be referred to the Legislative Committee, and if desired the two committees may meet in conference. If the Legislative Committee signifies its desire that the measure and report should be presented to Parliament, this is done, but the Legislative Committee is expressly given the right to withdraw the measure before it is so presented.

After it is presented, any member of either House of Parliament may propose a resolution that the measure shall be submitted to the Queen for her assent. Resolutions of both Houses are necessary, and on such resolutions being carried, the measure will be presented, and on the royal assent being signified it has the force and effect of an Act of Parliament.

## (6) DIOCESAN SYNODS

A diocesan synod consists of the bishop (who is president), a house of clergy, and a house of laity.

The house of clergy is composed of:

(1) *Ex-officio* members, who include suffragan and full-time assistant bishops; the dean or provost of the cathedral; the archdeacons; the chancellor of the diocese (if in holy orders); the chairman of the diocesan board of finance (if in holy orders); also the proctors elected from the diocese, and from any university in the diocese, to the Lower House of the Convocation of the province (excluding the registrar of the diocese if so elected);

(2) Members elected by the houses of clergy of the deanery synods of the diocese; and

(3) Co-opted members not exceeding five.

The house of laity is composed of:

(1) *Ex-officio* members, being the chancellor of the diocese (if not in holy orders); the chairman of the diocesan board of finance (if not in holy orders); and the members elected from the diocese to the House of Laity of the General Synod (excluding the registrar of the diocese if so elected);

(2) Members elected by the houses of laity of the deanery synods in the diocese;

(3) Co-opted members not exceeding five, who must be actual communicant members of the Church of England of age to vote at a Parliamentary election.

The bishop of the diocese has the right to nominate ten additional members of the synod, either clerical or lay, to be members of the appropriate house.

The rules for election of members from the deanery synods to the diocesan synods may be summarised as follows:

(i) The number of members (both clerical and lay) to be elected must be such as to secure that the total membership of the diocesan synod is not less than 150 nor more than 270 (or, for the purpose of the first two elections to the diocesan synod of the Diocese of London, 500).

(ii) The membership of the two houses of the diocesan synod must be approximately equal.

(iii) Subject to the foregoing, the diocesan synod determines, before each election, the number of members to be elected by each house of each deanery synod. In the case of an election by the house of clergy of a deanery synod, the number is related to the number of members of that house. In the case of an election by the house of laity of a deanery synod, the number is related to the total number of names on the rolls of the parishes in the deanery. But at least two members must be elected by each house of every deanery synod.

(iv) The electors in the house of clergy or in the house of laity of a deanery synod are all the members of that house other than co-opted members.

(v) Any clergyman who is a member of the deanery synod or is working or residing in the deanery is qualified to be elected by the house of clergy of a deanery synod.

(vi) Any lay person who is an actual communicant member of the Church of England of age to vote at a Parliamentary election, and whose name is entered on the roll of any parish in the deanery or who is a habitual worshipper at the cathedral church of the diocese and associated with the deanery, is qualified to be elected by the house of laity of a deanery synod.

(vii) The elections take place every three years,[1] and are held in June or July of the appropriate year.

The diocesan synod of any diocese has power to make a scheme for the variation of the rules relating to its own membership, in order to meet the special circumstances of the diocese, but the General Synod has (in effect) a right of veto over any such scheme.

The functions of a diocesan synod are stated in section 4(2) of the Synodical Government Measure 1969 as follows:

'(a) to consider matters concerning the Church of England and to make provision for such matters in relation to their [i.e. the synod's] diocese, and to consider and express their opinion on any other matters of religious or public interest;

(b) to advise the bishop on any matters on which he may consult the synod;

(c) to consider and express their opinion on any matters referred to them by the General Synod, and in particular to approve or disapprove provisions referred to them by the General Synod under Article 8 of the Constitution [i.e. provisions for

[1] The first elections were held in 1970 and the next are due in 1973.

which the approval of a majority of the dioceses is necessary: see pp. 11 and 12 *ante*]:

Provided that the functions referred to in paragraph (a) hereof shall not include the issue of any statement purporting to declare the doctrine of the Church on any question.'

It is the duty of the bishop to consult with the diocesan synod on matters of general concern and importance to the diocese.

Every diocesan synod must, by its standing orders, establish a body to be known as 'the bishop's Council and standing committee' with such membership as standing orders may provide. Subject to standing orders and to any directions of the synod, the above-mentioned functions of the synod may be discharged on its behalf by this body, but either the bishop or the body itself may require any matter to be referred to the synod.

The diocesan synod is enjoined to keep the deanery synods of the diocese informed of the policies and problems of the diocese and of the business which is to come before meetings of the diocesan synod, and it may delegate executive functions to deanery synods. It is also enjoined to keep itself informed, through the deanery synods, of events and opinion in the parishes, and to give opportunities at its meetings for discussing matters raised by deanery synods and parochial church councils.

In general, nothing is to be deemed to have the assent of the diocesan synod unless the three authorities which constitute the synod (i.e. the bishop and the two houses) have assented to it. But questions relating to the conduct of business are decided by a vote of the whole synod, and other questions will be similarly decided (the consent of the three authorities being assumed) unless ten members demand a vote by houses, or unless the bishop requires his distinct opinion to be recorded. In the case of a vote on a measure of the General Synod for which the approval of a majority of the dioceses in their synods is necessary,[1] the diocesan synod is deemed to have given its approval if both the two houses are in favour, even though the bishop is not (for the bishop has a sufficient voice in the matter when it is under consideration by the House of Bishops of the General Synod).

[1] See pp. 11, 12 *ante*.

## (7) DEANERY SYNODS

A deanery synod consists of a house of clergy and a house of laity.

The house of clergy is composed of:

(1) Clergymen beneficed in or licensed to any parish in the deanery;

(2) Clergymen licensed to institutions in the deanery under the Extra-Parochial Ministry Measure 1967 (e.g. university, hospital and prison chaplains);

(3) Clerical members of the General Synod or diocesan synod resident in the deanery;

(4) Such other clergy holding the bishop's licence and resident or working in the deanery as may be determined by or in accordance with a resolution of the diocesan synod.

The house of laity is composed of:

(1) Parochial representatives elected by the annual meetings of the parishes of the deanery;

(2) Lay members of the General Synod or diocesan synod whose names are entered on the roll of any parish in the deanery;

(3) Such other lay persons, being deaconesses or whole-time lay workers licensed by the bishop to work in any part of the deanery, as may be determined by or in accordance with a resolution of the diocesan synod.

Either house may co-opt additional members, but the members co-opted must not exceed five per cent of the total members of that house.

There are provisions for enabling a diocesan synod to provide for the representation, on an appropriate deanery synod, of the clergy of the cathedral church, and of lay persons who habitually worship at the cathedral church and whose names are not on the roll of any parish.

The rules for the election of parochial representatives to a deanery synod may be summarised as follows:

(i) The number to be elected must be such as to secure that the total membership of the synod is not more than 150 and, so far as practicable, not less than fifty; but the maximum of 150 may be exceeded for the purpose of securing that the house of laity is not less in number than the house of clergy.

(ii) Subject to the foregoing, the diocesan synod determines, before each election, the number to be elected by each parish to its deanery synod, such number being related to the number of names on the roll of the parish. Provision may be made for the separate representation of a district where there is a district church council.[1]

(iii) The elections take place (at the annual meetings of the parishes) every three years,[2] and the elected representatives hold office for a term of three years beginning with the first of June following their election.

The diocesan synod has power to make a scheme for the variation of the rules relating to the membership of deanery synods, in order to meet the special circumstances of the diocese or the deaneries, and to secure better representation of clergy or laity or both on the deanery synods, but the General Synod has (in effect) a right of veto over any such scheme.

The functions of a deanery synod are stated in section 5(3) of the Synodical Government Measure 1969 as follows:

'(a) to consider matters concerning the Church of England and to make provision for such matters in relation to their [i.e. the synod's] deanery, and to consider and express their opinion on any other matters of religious or public interest;

(b) to bring together the views of the parishes of the deanery on common problems, to discuss and formulate common policies on those problems, to foster a sense of community and interdependence among those parishes, and generally to promote in the deanery the whole mission of the church, pastoral, evangelistic, social and ecumenical;

(c) to make known and as far as appropriate put into effect any provision made by the diocesan synod;

(d) to consider the business of the diocesan synod and particularly any matters referred to that synod by the General Synod, and to sound parochial opinion whenever they are required or consider it appropriate to do so;

(e) to raise such matters as the deanery synod consider appropriate with the diocesan synod:

1 As to district church councils, see pp. 95, 123 *post*.
2 The first elections took place in 1970 and the next are due in 1973.

Provided that the functions referred to in paragraph (a) hereof shall not include the issue of any statement purporting to declare the doctrine of the Church on any question.'

Deanery synods are enjoined to exercise any functions which may be delegated to them by the diocesan synod in relation to the parishes of their deaneries, and in particular (if so delegated) the determination of parochial shares in 'quotas' allocated to the deaneries (meaning the amount to be subscribed to the expenditure authorised by the diocesan synod).

It is provided that the diocesan synod is to make rules for deanery synods. Such rules must provide that the rural dean and a member of the house of laity, elected by that house, shall be joint chairmen of the deanery synod; that there shall be a secretary of the deanery synod; that a specified minimum number of meetings shall be held in each year; that decisions shall be taken by a majority of members present and voting, except in cases where the rules provide for voting by houses; for a standing committee of the deanery synod; and for the preparation by the synod, and the circulation to all parochial church councils in the deanery, of a report of the synod's proceedings. The rules may also provide for other matters if the diocesan synod thinks fit.

## (8) GENERAL COMMENTS

Following the above statement of the effect of the Synodical Government Measure 1969, and of the scheme which it introduces, it may be helpful to summarise those features of the scheme which, in the light of the objects of the Measure as stated on p. 7 *ante*, may be regarded as of first importance.

(a) The transfer of the power to make canons from the Convocations to the General Synod is an undoubted simplification, since it has the effect of vesting the whole power of legislation in relation to the Church (other than the over-riding power of Parliament itself) in a single institution whose authority extends to the whole of England. It eliminates a possible source of confusion, and should therefore tend towards a sounder organisation. And it undoubtedly increases the sphere of lay participation in the affairs of the Church to a considerable degree.

(b) As a result of the transfer the Convocations have lost much of their former importance. But they still have certain functions and will continue to meet separately. Accordingly, the new power which each Convocation has, of adding a House of Laity to its existing two Houses for the purpose of all or any of its functions, may afford a further opportunity for lay participation; though it remains to be seen to what extent (if at all) this power will be exercised in practice.

(c) The drastic reduction in the size of the Lower Houses of the Convocations and (as a consequence thereof) in the size of the House of Clergy of the General Synod, together with the roughly equivalent reduction in the size of the House of Laity, may be expected to result in shorter and more incisive debates, more rapid decisions and action, and an all-round improvement in efficiency. It is perhaps worth mentioning that the House of Clergy as now constituted is a more democratic body than formerly, since the reduction was largely achieved by decreasing the number of dignitaries who were 'official' members. A larger proportion of the House now consists of proctors elected by the ordinary clergy of the dioceses.

(d) In most if not all dioceses, there has also been a reduction in size (resulting, it is to be hoped, in greater efficiency) at diocesan level. The composition of the former diocesan conferences varied considerably in different dioceses, but in many of them, all the parochial clergy were automatically members and there was at least one elected lay representative from every parish. In almost any diocese, this would produce a total membership far in excess of the maximum of 150 which now obtains for every diocesan synod except that of London.

(e) Yet another factor which should tend towards efficiency is the precise definition by the Measure of the functions of the diocesan and deanery synods. Previously, there was no similar definition of the functions of diocesan conferences or (where they existed) of ruri-decanal conferences.

(f) In drafting the Measure, great pains have obviously been taken to ensure good communications and the flow of information and ideas in both directions. One of the expressly stated functions of diocesan synods is to consider and express their opinions on matters referred to them by the General Synod; and a constant exchange of views and ideas between the diocesan synod on the one hand, and the deanery synods on the other hand, is also expressly provided for. Again, as between the deanery and the parishes, the deanery synod is enjoined to bring together the views of the parishes on common problems, to foster a scheme of community and interdependence among the parishes, and to sound parochial opinion.

As regards this last point, however, there is one important matter to be noted. The Measure plainly contemplates that communications should normally pass through a chain of organisations: from the General Synod to the diocesan synods, from the diocesan synod to the deanery synods, from the deanery synod to the parishes—and *vice versa*. There is little room for any direct communication from one organisation to another which is not immediately below or above it. In particular, communications between the diocesan synod and the parishes of the diocese must pass through the deanery synods.

On this aspect, there has been considerable criticism of the policy of the Measure. It has been pointed out, with truth, that parishes have, in the past, generally looked to the diocese, not to the rural deanery, for leadership and guidance. Indeed, so far at any rate as the laity are concerned, the rural deanery has hitherto assumed relatively little importance in the eyes of the churchmen in the parishes. And so it has been argued that the interposition of an elaborate deanery organisation between the diocese and the parishes not only renders the whole scheme of synodical government unnecessarily cumbrous, but also destroys a direct link which is both traditional and valuable.

The reason for establishing deanery synods was, of course, to avoid the necessity for direct parochial representation at diocesan level, which (it was envisaged) would render the diocesan synods over-large and unwieldy. One of the more radical suggestions made by critics for overcoming this difficulty is that the number of dioceses ought to be drastically increased, in order that their size may be sufficiently reduced to render direct parochial representation in the diocesan synods practicable and reasonable (and it has also been suggested that a reform on these lines would have spiritual as well as administrative advantages). A less radical proposal, favoured by other critics, has been that those existing dioceses which would prefer to have direct parochial representation at diocesan level should be at liberty to introduce it by appropriate amendments of the constitutions of their diocesan synods; it is likely that several of the less populous and more rural dioceses would avail themselves of such a liberty if they were granted it.

In fact, as matters now stand under the Measure, any diocesan synod has power to introduce a scheme for the variation of the rules laid down by the Measure concerning the membership of the synod; and presumably any such scheme could provide for direct representation of the parishes in the synod. But schemes under this power are subject to veto by the General Synod, and there is a strong possibility that any scheme which deviated so far from the norm which the Measure contemplates would in fact be vetoed.

How much substance there is in the above-mentioned criticisms can only be shown by practical experience of the working of the Measure.

# CHAPTER III

# THE COURTS OF THE CHURCH

(1) **Diocesan Courts**—(2) **Provincial Courts**—(3) **Court of Ecclesiastical Causes Reserved**—(4) **Proceedings for Ecclesiastical Offences.**

## (1) DIOCESAN COURTS

The law relating to ecclesiastical courts and the trial of ecclesiastical cases has been much revised, and to a large extent codified, by the Ecclesiastical Jurisdiction Measure 1963.

Under that Measure (as previously), every archbishop (in his diocesan capacity) and every diocesan bishop has a court for the trial of ecclesiastical matters arising in his diocese. In the Diocese of Canterbury this court is known as the Commissary Court and elsewhere as the Consistory Court. The judge of the court is, in Canterbury, styled the 'Commissary-General' and in other dioceses the 'Chancellor'. In this book, the expressions 'consistory court' and 'chancellor' are intended to cover the diocesan court and its judge in every diocese including Canterbury.

The chancellor is appointed by the bishop. He must be at least thirty years old and either a barrister of seven years' standing or a person who has held high judicial office; and if the bishop appoints a layman, he must satisfy himself that the appointee is a communicant. If the chancellor's appointment is confirmed by the dean and chapter or the cathedral chapter of the cathedral church (as in practice it invariably is), he remains in office until death or resignation, subject to a power for the bishop to remove him if the Upper House of the Convocation of the province resolves that he is incapable of acting or unfit to act.

The status of the bishop in his own court depends upon the terms of the patent appointing the chancellor. In some cases the bishop expressly reserves to himself the power to sit and try certain cases or classes of cases. But except so far as this power is reserved, the chancellor is the sole judge, and indeed may try cases to which the bishop himself is a party.

The consistory court is the court of first instance for the trial of faculty cases (as to which see the next chapter), and also for the trial of proceedings against priests or deacons for offences not involving any matter of doctrine, ritual or ceremonial.

## (2) PROVINCIAL COURTS

The provincial courts of Canterbury and York are known respectively as the Court of Arches (or Arches Court of Canterbury) and the Chancery Court of York.

There are five judges of each court. One of them, who is a judge of both courts, is appointed by the two archbishops subject to the approval of the Queen: in the Province of Canterbury he is styled 'Dean of the Arches', and in that of York 'Auditor'. Of the other four judges in each court, two are clergymen appointed by the prolocutor of the Lower House of Convocation of the relevant province; and two are communicant laymen possessing judicial experience, appointed by the Chairman of the House of Laity of the General Synod after consultation with the Lord Chancellor.

Each provincial court is the court of appeal from the consistory courts within the province in faculty cases not involving matters of doctrine, ritual or ceremonial (for the hearing of which cases the Dean of the Arches or Auditor sits alone); also in proceedings against priests and deacons for offences not involving such matters (for the hearing of which all five judges sit).

In faculty cases there is a further appeal from the provincial court to the Judicial Committee of the Privy Council.

## (3) COURT OF ECCLESIASTICAL CAUSES RESERVED

This court consists of five judges appointed by the Queen. Two of them are persons who hold or have held high judicial office and who are communicants, and the other three are persons who are, or have been, diocesan bishops.

This court is the court of first instance for proceedings against the clergy for offences against the laws ecclesiastical involving matters of doctrine, ritual or ceremonial. It is also the court of appeal from consistory courts in faculty cases involving such matters. In either class of case, there is a final appeal from the

Court of Ecclesiastical Causes Reserved to a 'Commission of Review,' consisting of three lay Lords of Appeal who are communicants, and two diocesan bishops who are members of the House of Lords.

## (4) PROCEEDINGS FOR ECCLESIASTICAL OFFENCES

There are special provisions in the Measure of 1963 as regards the trial of archbishops and bishops for ecclesiastical offences, but space does not permit their detailed consideration. Something, however, should be said of the nature of proceedings against priests and deacons.

All such proceedings commence with a complaint laid before the registrar of the diocese. Any person authorised by the bishop may lay a complaint. A complaint may also be laid, in the case of an incumbent or of an assistant curate, or of a curate-in-charge of a conventional district, by six or more persons of full age whose names are on the electoral roll; or, in the case of an assistant curate, by his incumbent.

The procedure following upon a complaint differs according as to whether any matter of doctrine, ritual or ceremonial is involved. If no such matter is involved, the bishop, after giving both the accused and the complainant the opportunity of a private interview, may decide either to take no further steps (and thereby to put an end to the proceedings) or to refer the matter to an 'examiner', who is selected for the purpose from a panel of examiners consisting of qualified lawyers. It is the function of the examiner to inquire into the complaint and to decide whether there is a case for the accused to answer. If he decides that there is no such case, that ends the proceedings. But if he decides that there is such a case, he must specify the alleged offence in his report, and the next step is for the bishop to nominate a fit person to promote a complaint against the accused in the consistory court. At the hearing in that court, the chancellor (or a duly qualified person appointed by him with the bishop's consent to take his place) sits as judge, with four assessors (two clerical and two lay) appointed from a panel of assessors to act as jury. If as a result of the trial the accused is found guilty, he is sentenced by the bishop, who may pronounce on the accused such of the censures mentioned below as he thinks fit.

The offences for which a priest or deacon may be put on trial under the procedure outlined above are: (i) conduct unbecoming the office and work of a clerk in holy orders, and (ii) serious, persistent, or continuous neglect of duty.

At any time after the laying of the original complaint, the bishop, after consulting the complainant and with the consent of the accused, may pronounce a censure forthwith, and the proceedings are then at an end. In effect, the accused's consent is treated as a plea of guilty.

Any of the following censures can be pronounced by the bishop against an accused who is found guilty or who consents, viz. deprivation from existing preferment, coupled with disqualification from future preferment except on certain conditions; inhibition, i.e. disqualification for a specified period from exercising the functions of his order; suspension from his preferment for a specified period; monition, i.e. an order to do or refrain from doing a specified act; or rebuke. If a sentence of deprivation is pronounced, the bishop may also (subject to a right for the accused to appeal to the archbishop)[1] depose the accused from holy orders, and any such deposition can subsequently be reversed only by a free pardon from the Crown.

There are provisions in the Measure for the pronouncement of censure of deprivation on a priest or deacon as a result of a finding against him in a secular court, without any further trial in a church court. These provisions apply if a priest or deacon is sentenced to imprisonment on being convicted of a criminal offence, or if an affiliation order is made against him, or if he is found in a matrimonial suit to have committed any of certain moral offences.

If a complaint against a priest or deacon involves a matter of doctrine, ritual or ceremonial, the bishop, after giving both the accused and the complainant an opportunity of being interviewed in private, must decide either that no further step is to be taken, or to refer the complaint to a specially constituted committee for inquiry. Such committee consists of one member of the Upper House and two members of the Lower House of the Convocation of the province, and two chancellors of dioceses in the province. No further steps are to be taken in the matter if the committee,

[1] If the decision is an archbishop's, the appeal lies to the other archbishop.

C

after due inquiry, decides that there is no case for the accused to answer, or alternatively that, although there is a case for him to answer, the offence is too trivial to warrant further proceedings, or that there were extenuating circumstances, or that further proceedings would not be in the interests of the Church. If, however, the committee recommend further proceedings, the Upper House of Convocation has to nominate a fit person to promote a complaint against the accused in the Court of Ecclesiastical Causes Reserved, and the case is brought before that court accordingly. There is provision whereby the court, in the trial of any case, will have the assistance of three to five expert advisers. If the court finds the accused guilty, it decides on and pronounces the appropriate censure; but no censure more severe than monition can be pronounced in the case of a first offence.

All decisions in the Court of Ecclesiastical Causes Reserved are by a majority of the judges.

# CHAPTER IV

## FACULTIES

The consecrated buildings and lands situated within a diocese are in the ultimate guardianship of the bishop, who exercises his authority in this respect through his chancellor. In consequence the legal proceeding known as the application for and the granting of a faculty is necessary for the sanction of alterations in a consecrated building or its contents, or in a churchyard or other consecrated burial ground or its contents.

The faculty jurisdiction extends to unconsecrated land which forms, or is part of, the curtilage of a consecrated church (Faculty Jurisdiction Measure 1964, section 7). And it may also be extended, by an order of the bishop, and during the period specified in such order, to any building which he has licensed for public worship (section 6).

The petition for a faculty is lodged in the consistory court of the diocese, before the chancellor as judge of that court. It is usually made in the name of the incumbent and churchwardens, but this is not necessary, since any person who is regarded by the law as having an interest is entitled either to apply for or to oppose the grant of a faculty; and for this purpose all the following persons are regarded as having an interest, viz. the parishioners, persons who though not resident in the parish are on its electoral roll, and the archdeacon;[1] and also in some types of case, certain other persons as well.

The object of obtaining a faculty is to ensure that the work proposed to be done shall not subsequently be interfered with, for if anything is done without the grant of a faculty, it is open to any parishioner, or other person having an interest, to apply for a faculty authorising the removal of the work. In such a case the incumbent and churchwardens, or any other person or persons also having an interest, may lodge a cross-petition for a

---

[1] See Faculty Jurisdiction Measure 1964, section 2. If the archdeaconry is vacant, or if the archdeacon is incapacitated or unable or unwilling to act, the bishop may appoint another person to act in his place.

confirmatory faculty authorising retrospectively what is sought to be removed.

Trivial additions to the church or its furniture, e.g. alms-boxes or hassocks, do not require a faculty.

As regards the churchyard, no faculty is necessary for the burial of a body; on the other hand, a body cannot be removed from consecrated ground for burial elsewhere without a faculty. For the erection of a monument, a faculty is required in strict law, but usually this is not insisted on in practice, and the incumbent's approval is regarded as sufficient. If he refuses approval, the person desirous of erecting the monument can petition for a faculty to reverse his decision.

Repairs necessary in the ordinary course of upkeep do not require a faculty, but it is not always easy to decide whether any particular proposal amounts only to a matter of repair. The decision whether a faculty is necessary in any given case rests with the chancellor, and it is desirable that any question of doubt should be referred to him.

No faculty may be granted for anything illegal, e.g. because it has a superstitious purpose, or because it would be inconsistent with the sacred purposes for which the building or land was consecrated. But within the limits of legality, the consistory court has an extremely wide discretion to give or refuse a faculty for almost any sort of work or innovation. This discretion must, however, be exercised judicially and for proper reasons. Certain conditions and restrictions are imposed by the Faculty Jurisdiction Measure 1964 on the grant of a faculty for the demolition or partial demolition of a church.

The jurisdiction of the consistory court does not extend to those cathedrals where the dean and not the bishop is the ordinary, nor to those cathedrals which are also parish churches, the cathedral statutes of which place the church outside such jurisdiction.

There is in every diocese an Advisory Committee whose function it is to assist the chancellor on the one hand and the parishioners on the other. These committees usually consist of experts in architecture, archaeology, and art, who know the diocese and its churches. They are ready to advise the parishioners before the proposals are embodied in a petition for a faculty, and the chancellor on any proposals submitted to him. The advisory committee system has justified itself by results, and considerable attention is given to the committees by most chancellors. A Central Council for the Care of Churches also exists, the purpose of which is to co-ordinate the work of the diocesan committees and to advise in cases which present special difficulty.

In a simple case, where there is no opposition, a chancellor may, and commonly does, grant a faculty without a hearing in court. But if in his opinion the case involves some legal or other difficulty or complication, he is likely to direct a hearing in open court; and he will always do so if the petition is opposed.

Under the Faculty Jurisdiction Measure 1964, section 12, the archdeacon is empowered to issue a certificate for certain types of work which will take effect in lieu of a faculty, provided that application is made to him by the incumbent and churchwardens of the parish, and is supported by a resolution of the parochial church council, and is unopposed. The works in question are:

(a) Repairs to a church not involving substantial change in its structure nor affecting its appearance;
(b) Repairs to the contents of a church not materially affecting their nature or appearance;
(c) Redecoration of a church or its contents;
(d) Any alteration in an existing heating system not involving a substantial change in the church's appearance.

The chancellor may direct the same procedure with regard to any other application which, in his opinion, is unlikely to give rise to any controversy or dissatisfaction in the parish and is not important enough to justify the expense of faculty proceedings.

CHAPTER V

# THE PARISH

(1) Ancient Parishes—(2) New and Altered Parishes—(3) Unions of Benefices and Parishes—(4) Team and Group Ministries—(5) Conventional
Districts—(6) Sharing of Church Buildings—(7) Guild Churches.

## (1) ANCIENT PARISHES

A parish is an area committed to the incumbent by the bishop
for the cure (i.e. care) of souls. Within the parish the incumbent
is, under the bishop, supreme, but his supremacy is constitutional and not arbitrary. He is the bishop's deputy for most
purposes within the parish, and his 'cure' is exercised to the
exclusion of other clergy.

The growth of the parochial system was a gradual process.
While the bishop is the incumbent, and the cathedral is the parish
church, of the whole diocese, and the only essential 'parson' for
the existence of a diocese is the bishop with his cathedral church,
it became necessary at an early stage for him to have assistants
in his ministrations. It may be mentioned that the term 'parson'
is really a corrupt abbreviation of *ecclesiae persona* or 'ecclesiastical person'. The first stage of parochial development was for
the bishop to ordain clergy to assist him in the diocese, who were
then sent out by him to preach and administer the sacraments in
any district to which he might assign them. As yet no churches
existed, and the clergy resided with the bishop where his *cathedra*
or 'seat' was.

In course of time, churches were built and endowed, and they
required clergy to minister in them. The person who built the
church usually nominated a layman for ordination to the cure,
or a priest to perform the duties there. Very often the founder
of the church would be the local lord of the manor. In this growth
of church buildings we see the beginnings of the right to present
clergy to incumbencies, a right vested in some person, not
necessarily the bishop, which is familiar at the present day. The

30

person in whom the right is vested is now known as the 'patron', and his status is historically derived from the 'lord' who built a church on his demesne, and nominated the man of his choice as the minister of that church. The country gradually became covered with churches, each of which served a district which coincided more or less with a political area, and these districts are the predecessors of the parishes of modern times.

While this was the normal process, it sometimes happened that the bishop would assign a district to a church, and place one of his clergy there.

But, however the local conditions varied, the priest who served each church was called a 'curate', as a person to whom the cure of souls was delegated. The districts assigned to churches came to be called parishes; and by the end of the thirteenth century practically the whole realm had been divided up into parishes, and the ecclesiastical units so formed are now termed '*ancient* parishes'.

As was to be expected, however, changed circumstances, especially increases in the population of urban and suburban areas, demanded modifications in the scheme of ancient parishes. From the early nineteenth century onwards, a number of Acts of Parliament, notably the Church Building Acts 1818 to 1884 and the New Parishes Acts 1843 to 1884, were passed to enable new parishes or districts to be created where they were required. For all practical purposes, all these Acts were repealed and replaced by the New Parishes Measure 1943, the relevant provisions of which have now themselves been repealed and replaced by the Pastoral Measure 1968.

Numerous parishes have been created over the years under these various statutes and are now in existence. Although they are in fact modern ecclesiastical units, the law relating to them is, for practical purposes, virtually the same as the law relating to ancient parishes.

## (2) NEW AND ALTERED PARISHES

Until the New Parishes Measure 1943 unified and simplified the law, there was a bewildering variety of provisions, laying down different conditions and procedures, in relation to the creation of new parishes. Both the Measure of 1943, and the Acts which it replaced, made provision in certain circumstances (where for some reason the immediate creation of a new parish was deemed inexpedient) for the creation of 'districts' of various sorts. The status of all these districts was inferior to that of fully-fledged parishes. Although they enjoyed a considerable degree of independence, they remained dependent on their parent parishes for certain purposes: e.g. the church or chapel (if any) of a district was not normally licensed for marriages, so that recourse was necessary to the church of the parent parish for the publication of banns and for the marriage ceremony itself.

Apart from any statute, the law recognised a type of district, known as a 'parochial chapelry', if the area in question contained a chapel to which (and not the parish church) the inhabitants customarily resorted for spiritual services such as baptisms and burials, and whose minister received the customary fees as of right for his services. Under the Church Building Act 1845 (until repealed by the New Parishes Measure 1943), a similar type of district, known as a 'district chapelry', came into being where, in accordance with the Act, a definite area or district was assigned to a chapel-of-ease with the consent of the bishop.

Under the New Parishes Measure 1943, if a scheme was made in accordance with the Measure for the purpose of constituting a defined area as a new parish, and if at the time of making the scheme the area contained no consecrated church suitable to be the parish church, the area in question became forthwith 'a separate district for spiritual purposes'; such a district acquired full parochial status as soon as a church within it had been both consecrated and approved by the Church Commissioners as suitable.

By the Pastoral Measure 1968, section 86, all the various types of district referred to above and all other ecclesiastical 'districts' of any sort, but excluding 'conventional districts' (which are considered later in this chapter), were converted into parishes as from the commencement of the Measure, the minister of the district becoming the vicar of the parish without any further process or form of law.

The only statutory provisions now in force for the creation of new parishes, or the alteration of existing ones, are those contained in the Pastoral Measure 1968 itself. This Measure provides for the establishment in every diocese of a Pastoral Committee, and for the making by the Church Commissioners of 'pastoral schemes', based on proposals submitted by the Pastoral Committee with the approval of the bishop; any such scheme takes effect on its being confirmed by Order in Council. At various stages in the proceedings leading to the making and confirmation of a scheme, there are provisions for ascertaining the views of 'interested parties' (who include, amongst others, all incumbents, patrons and parochial church councils liable to be concerned); for giving notice, both in the press and to particular persons, of the objects of the intended scheme and of its submission for confirmation; and for dealing with any written representations which may be received with respect to it. Any person who has made written representations with respect to a scheme, and whose objections have not been met, has a right of appeal to the Judicial Committee of the Privy Council; and the scheme will not be confirmed until the appeal has been decided.

Amongst the matters for which a pastoral scheme may provide are the following, viz.: the creation, by union or otherwise, of new benefices[1] or parishes; the dissolution of existing benefices or parishes; and the alteration of the areas of existing benefices or parishes (including the transfer of a parish from one benefice to another) or the definition of their boundaries.

There are wide powers in the Measure for enabling a scheme to deal with any churches in the area to which it extends. Generally speaking, where a scheme creates a new parish or alters an existing parish, any church in the new or altered parish may be designated by the scheme as the parish church. But if there is only one church in the new or altered parish which is an 'existing parish church' (i.e. was a parish church immediately before the scheme became operative) that church will be the parish church unless the scheme expressly substitutes another; and again, if the new or altered parish contains no 'existing parish church', but does contain a church which the Church Commissioners have already approved as suitable to be a parish church, the church so approved will be the parish church on the coming into operation of the scheme or on its subsequent consecration. Finally, if a new or altered parish contains two or more 'existing parish churches', the scheme may designate two or more churches (not necessarily the same ones) to be the parish churches of the

[1] As to the meaning of 'benefice', see p. 35 *post.*

new or altered parish; each of the churches so designated will be a parish church of the whole parish for all purposes, including the solemnisation of marriages.

A scheme may create a new parish with full parochial status although there will be no parish church when the scheme comes into operation. In such a case, and in any other case of a parish having no parish church, as soon as a church within the parish is approved by the Church Commissioners and is consecrated, it becomes the parish church. Meanwhile, the bishop has power to license one or more buildings or parts of buildings for public worship; he may also designate any building or part of a building so licensed as the 'parish centre of worship', whereupon, so long as the designation remains in force, it is deemed to be the parish church for all legal purposes, including the solemnisation of marriages. (This does not affect the right, under the Marriage Act 1949, of parishioners intending to be married to resort for the purpose to the church of an adjoining parish until their own parish has an actual parish church. Meanwhile, they have an option in the matter.)

A scheme may substitute for a parish church another church in the parish which has been approved by the Church Commissioners for the purpose, whether or not the parish is otherwise affected by the scheme.

Any church in an area affected by a scheme which is deprived by the scheme of the status of a parish church, or which does not acquire that status under the scheme, will either continue in use as a chapel-of-ease, or be declared redundant by the scheme. The Measure lays down a complicated procedure for dealing with redundant churches which it is beyond the scope of this book to describe in detail. As a rule, unless there is some suitable use to which a redundant church can be put or for which it can be disposed of by sale or otherwise, it is liable eventually to be demolished; but there are special provisions concerning the preservation of churches of historical or architectural interest.

Some of the powers conferred by the Measure may be exercised by a 'pastoral order' instead of by a pastoral scheme. The procedure for making an order is relatively simple: the order is proposed by the Church Commissioners and made by the bishop; no confirmation by Order in Council is necessary, and there is no appeal to the Judicial Committee of the Privy Council. But any proposals for the creation or dissolution or union of benefices or parishes, or for transferring any church used for public worship from any benefice or parish, can only be given effect to by a scheme.

### (3) UNIONS OF BENEFICES AND PARISHES

Within the context of the parochial ministry, a benefice may be defined as the office of the rector or vicar (i.e. of the incumbent) of a parish. Thus a union of benefices, without more, entails simply the concentration of both or all of the incumbencies of two or more parishes, as one office or benefice, in the hands of one incumbent. The identity of the parishes themselves is not affected; each of them remains a separate parish, with its own parish church and parochial organisation. The only legal link between them is that their combined incumbencies have become a single office, held by a single incumbent whom they share.

A union of parishes necessarily involves a union of the benefices of the parishes concerned. But it also entails the loss, by each of those parishes, of its separate identity, and the merger of both or all of them into a single new united parish.

Immediately before the coming into force of the Pastoral Measure 1968, unions were governed, in the case of benefices situated wholly or partly in the City of London, by the Union of Benefices Act 1860, and in other cases by the Union of Benefices Measures 1923 to 1952. But both the Act of 1860 and the Measures last mentioned have now been repealed by the Pastoral Measure 1968; and any proposed union of benefices or parishes, wherever situated, can now only be effected by a pastoral scheme under the provisions outlined above. The Measure of 1968 contains full powers for the purpose, and in particular declares that a pastoral scheme providing for the union of two or more benefices may provide for uniting all the parishes within the area of the new benefice, or for uniting some but not all of them, or may leave them as separate parishes.

### (4) TEAM AND GROUP MINISTRIES

In recent years, in various parts of the country, there have been experiments based on the idea of an association of clergymen co-operating in the running of an area considerably larger than a normal parish.

In different places there may be different reasons for such an experiment. In some areas (mostly rural) it can be an effective method of coping with a shortage of clergy, by deploying the available clergy to the best advantage. Elsewhere, in thickly populated built-up areas (such as a 'new town' or a suburb of recent growth) a considerable modification of the ordinary parochial system may be thought desirable, on account of the difficulty of dividing an area of this sort into parishes of normal size, each capable of existing as a separate community with a life of its own. Yet another possible advantage of these arrangements is the scope and opportunity they can offer to clergy with specialist training or talents.

The Pastoral Measure 1968 affords for the first time a legal basis for team and group ministries, by enacting that a pastoral scheme may provide for the establishment of a ministry of either of these two sorts. It also contains provisions defining and safeguarding the status of the clergy engaged in them.

A team ministry is a ministry which normally covers the area of a single benefice, although it may be extended to the area of two or more benefices if and so long as all such benefices are held in plurality by the same incumbent. Any benefice concerned may of course, as a result of a union of benefices, contain any number of separate parishes. Under the provisions of the Measure, the incumbent of the benefice or benefices is styled 'rector', and is the principal member of the team. The other clergy in the team are styled 'vicars'.

A group ministry is a ministry covering two or more benefices with different incumbents, the general principle being that each incumbent will, besides attending to his own benefice, assist the incumbents of the other benefices.

Either a team or a group ministry may be dissolved by a subsequent pastoral scheme.

Broadly, the contrast between a team ministry and a group ministry is that the former operates on the basis of a team under a leader (the incumbent or 'rector'), whilst the latter is a partnership of equals, each of whom is an incumbent with primacy in the area of his own benefice.

Both types of ministry are primarily concerned with the

organisation of clerical man-power within a particular area; and the status and duties of the participating clergy will be more particularly considered in the next chapter. But in relation to both of them, the Measure also contains special provisions as regards such matters as patronage and parochial church councils, and these provisions will be noted, later in this book, under the appropriate heads.

## (5) CONVENTIONAL DISTRICTS

Conventional districts are sometimes formed in anticipation of their subsequently becoming distinct parishes: they are un-affected by the Pastoral Measure 1968. They are not parishes, but merely areas which are placed, with the consent of the incumbent and the bishop, under the care of a 'curate-in-charge' upon whom devolves the responsibility for the cure of souls in the district. The arrangement requires renewal with every change in the incumbency of the parish in which the district lies.

## (6) SHARING OF CHURCH BUILDINGS

The Sharing of Church Buildings Act 1969 was passed with the general object of facilitating agreements (termed 'sharing agreements') for the sharing and use of church buildings by different Christian bodies. Where a parish or other church of the Church of England is the subject-matter of a sharing agreement, or where the competent authorities of the Church of England enter into a sharing agreement in relation to a church belonging to some other Christian body, or to a church proposed to be built, this is likely to have a considerable effect on the life and organisation of the parish concerned.

The Churches which may be parties to a sharing agreement include the Church of England, the Roman Catholic Church, and all the principal Free Church bodies. Any two or more of such Churches may enter into a sharing agreement with respect to any existing or proposed church building or buildings. In the case of the Church of England, the Diocesan Board of Finance of the diocese concerned, and the incumbent and parochial church council of the parish concerned, are necessary parties to any sharing agreement; and the consent of the bishop and the

Pastoral Committee of the diocese must also be obtained. The necessary parties to a sharing agreement on behalf of the Roman Catholic Church or any Free Church are such persons as may be determined by the appropriate authority of that Church.

As regards ownership, a sharing agreement may provide for the shared building or buildings to be owned by one only of the sharing Churches or to be jointly owned by all or some of them. But this is subject to the qualification that an existing consecrated church of the Church of England must remain in the sole ownership of the Church of England, unless authority is given by a pastoral scheme to provide for joint ownership by the Church of England and another Church or Churches. An unconsecrated church building which is the subject-matter of a sharing agreement is not permitted to be consecrated, unless under the agreement it is in the sole ownership of the Church of England. And any church building which is shared by the Church of England under a sharing agreement may only become or remain a parish church if, under the agreement, it is in the sole ownership of the Church of England; but even if it is not in such sole ownership, its designation as a 'parish centre of worship'[1] is permissible.

A sharing agreement must make provision (amongst other things) for determining the extent to which any church building to which it applies is to be available for worship in accordance with the forms and practice of the sharing Churches; and for dealing with financial obligations as to repairs, furnishings, etc. It must also contain appropriate provisions for its own termination.

## (7) GUILD CHURCHES

The status of 'guild church' is peculiar to the City of London, and is the creation of the City of London (Guild Churches) Act 1952 (a private Act). Although guild churches are not parish churches, the Act gives them a comparable organisation and it is convenient to mention them briefly here.

The status was devised as a method of dealing with the special circumstances obtaining in the City, where on the one hand there are far more churches than are necessary for the needs of resident

[1] See p. 34 *ante.*

Sunday worshippers; but on the other hand, there is on working days a vast influx of non-residents who are proper objects of pastoral care, and many of whom are attendants at week-day services in City churches.

A number of former parish churches in the City have been converted into guild churches under the Act of 1952, or the City of London (Guild Churches) Act 1960 (which amended it in certain respects). As such, they no longer have the status of parish churches; nevertheless, they are wholly independent of the parishes in which they are respectively situated. Each guild church has a minister, who is appointed by a patron, is licensed by the bishop, is free from any control by the incumbent of the parish, and is entitled to the style of 'vicar'. His period of office, initially five years, may be extended from time to time for additional periods of three years each. In relation to the guild church and its churchyard he has the same rights and duties as those of a parish incumbent in relation to the parish church and church-yard; but he is under no liability to provide Sunday services. An assistant curate may also be appointed.

Provision is made for churchwardens and sidesmen of a guild church, for a guild church electoral roll, and for a guild church council, which is analogous to a parochial church council and similarly composed.

# CHAPTER VI

# THE PAROCHIAL CLERGY

---

(1) **The Incumbent:** (*a*) **Rectors and Vicars;** (*b*) **Institution and Collation;** (*c*) **Induction;** (*d*) **Conduct of Services;** (*e*) **Incumbent's other Duties;** (*f*) **Enforcement of Duties;** (*g*) **Avoidance of Benefice—(2) The Unbeneficed Clergy—(3) Members of Team and Group Ministries.**

---

## (1) THE INCUMBENT

### (a) *Rectors and Vicars*

The smallest normal unit of organisation is, as has been already indicated, the parish, at the head of which is the incumbent, who has the cure of souls therein, and is either a 'rector' or a 'vicar'. The difference between a rector and a vicar is historical rather than practical. Briefly, it may be said that where the whole of the tithe and glebe were attached to the benefice for the maintenance of the minister, that benefice is a rectory; in any other case, the benefice is a vicarage.

Previously to the Pastoral Measure 1968, there was a third class of benefice called a perpetual curacy, which arose where the incumbent was neither a rector, nor was an endowment provided out of the income of the rectory for his maintenance; the benefices of new ecclesiastical parishes were as a rule perpetual curacies. But the Measure has now converted all perpetual curacies into vicarages. The incumbencies of districts converted by the same Measure into parishes are likewise vicarages.

On a union, by a pastoral scheme, of two or more benefices one of which is a rectory, the new benefice created by the union is a rectory. And on the dissolution of a rectory under a pastoral scheme, otherwise than as a result of a union of benefices, the benefice in the area of which the residence of the rector of the dissolved benefice is situated is likewise a rectory. But except in those two cases, or in the case of a team ministry, every new benefice created by a pastoral scheme is a vicarage.

In the context of team ministries, the expressions 'rector' and 'vicar' have special meanings which are considered later in this chapter.

### (b) *Institution and Collation*

An incumbent is 'presented' to the bishop by the patron of the benefice, except where the bishop himself is the patron. He is put in possession of the cure of souls by the bishop by a process known as institution, or, where the bishop is patron, as collation.

Under the Benefices Act 1898, the bishop can refuse to institute a presentee if, at the date of the vacancy, not more than one year has elapsed since a transfer of the advowson (unless it be proved that the transfer was not effected in view of the probability of a vacancy within the year); or on the ground that at the date of presentation not more than three years have elapsed since the presentee was made a deacon; or on the ground of the unfitness of the presentee by reason of physical or mental infirmity or incapacity, or serious pecuniary embarrassment, or for any of the moral reasons specified in the Act; or on the ground of his having, with reference to the presentation, been knowingly party or privy to any transaction or agreement which is invalid under the Act.

If the bishop refuses to institute on any of these grounds, the patron or the presentee has a right of appeal to a special court constituted by the Act.

Before the incumbent is instituted, the notice of the bishop's intention to admit[1] must be sent to the churchwardens and affixed by them to the church door, where it must remain for a calendar month, and the presentee must subscribe the declaration of assent and the declaration against simony, and must take the oaths of allegiance and of canonical obedience. These preliminaries are also necessary before collation.

### (c) *Induction*

The incumbent is put into possession of the temporalities of the benefice by the process known as 'induction', which is performed by the archdeacon on the mandate of the bishop. Induction is sometimes performed by the rural dean, but it is doubtful

[1] See p. 69 *post.*

D

whether he can act except as the archdeacon's deputy and on his mandate. In practice, institution and induction take place usually at a service held at the parish church, but this is not necessary, and an institution can be made even at a place outside the diocese. But induction should always be after institution, and should not precede it.

On the first Sunday upon which the new incumbent officiates in the church he reads the Thirty-nine Articles of Religion and makes the declaration of assent in the presence of the congregation.[1] The churchwardens usually certify that this requirement has been duly complied with.

The incumbent, once put in possession of his benefice, has within it, subject only to the rights of the bishop and his officers, the exclusive duty of ministering and the exclusive rights to the emoluments appertaining to the cure.

### (d) *Conduct of Services*

The incumbent is responsible for the performance of divine service in his parish. In the absence of reasonable hindrance, he is bound to provide that Morning and Evening Prayer daily, and on appointed days the Litany, are said in the church, or one of the churches, of which he is the minister; also (unless dispensed by the bishop) that, in every parish church within his cure, Morning and Evening Prayer are said or sung at least on all Sundays and principal feast days, and on Ash Wednesday and Good Friday. Unless dispensed by the bishop, he must celebrate, or cause to be celebrated, the Holy Communion on all Sundays and greater feast days and on Ash Wednesday; and he must administer the sacraments and other rites (including baptisms, marriages and funerals) as occasion requires. Except for reasonable cause approved by the bishop, he must preach or cause to be preached a sermon at least once each Sunday (see Canons B 11, C 24).

The incumbent, in addition to the services which he is bound to hold in church, may hold services at other times or in other places. He may not, however, celebrate the Holy Communion anywhere except in church and in ministering to the sick except with the bishop's permission.

[1] In special circumstances, the bishop can appoint some other Sunday.

As to forms of services, the incumbent is bound to observe the orders, rites and ceremonies prescribed in the Prayer Book, and no other, except so far as be ordered by lawful authority. The precise extent of the exception has been considerably disputed in the past, but the problem has now to some extent been mitigated, though by no means finally settled, by the provisions of the Prayer Book (Alternative and Other Services) Measure 1965.

The main purpose of that Measure was to legalise the use of experimental forms of service alternative to those prescribed by the Prayer Book. Any particular alternative form may be approved in the appropriate manner for a period or successive periods not exceeding seven years for any one period; but the total maximum period of experimentation, as regards each particular service prescribed by the Prayer Book, is fourteen years from the time when an alternative form of that service was first approved. The approval required was originally that of each House of each Convocation, and of the House of Laity of the Church Assembly, with a two-thirds majority in each case; now, under the Synodical Government Measure 1969, it is the approval of each House of the General Synod with a like majority. Provision is also made whereby a preliminary trial may be given to any draft alternative form of service, approved for this purpose by the General Synod, in any such church or churches as the bishop may arrange, with the incumbent's approval in each case; but strict time-limits are set on the exercise of this power, and in particular no one draft form of service may be used under it for a longer period than two years. The use under any provision of the Measure of any particular alternative form or draft alternative form of service, in any church in a parish, is subject to the agreement of the parochial church council, lacking which its use is unauthorised.

Alternative forms of the services of Morning and Evening Prayer and of Holy Communion, and of certain of the occasional offices, have received approval under these provisions, and are at present widely in use.

The Measure of 1965 also contains powers under which (in effect) the Convocations, or failing any authorisation by them, the bishop of a diocese, may authorise special forms of service for occasions for which the Prayer Book makes no provision. In respect of any such occasion for which neither the Convocations nor the bishop have authorised a form of service, the minister concerned may use any form of service he considers suitable. But the exercise of the power conferred on a bishop or a minister by these provisions is subject to any regulations from time to time made by the Convocation of the province. The functions of the Convocations under these provisions have not been affected by the Synodical Government Measure 1969.

The Measure of 1965 also empowers a minister in his discretion to make variations not of substantial importance in any form of service prescribed by the Prayer Book or authorised by the Measure itself, according to particular circumstances.

The dress of a minister at divine service is laid down by the Vestures of Ministers Measure 1964 and Canon B 8. At Morning and Evening Prayer he is to wear cassock, surplice and scarf; and for occasional offices cassock, surplice and either scarf or stole. At the Holy Communion he is enjoined to wear with the cassock either a surplice with scarf or stole, or a surplice or alb with stole and cope, or an alb with the customary vestments. On any appropriate occasion he may wear a cope; and when he wears a scarf, he may also wear, if a graduate, the hood of his degree. But he is not to change the form of vesture in use in the church in which he officiates without first ascertaining, by consultation with the parochial church council, that such change will be acceptable; in case of disagreement he is to refer the matter to the bishop, whose direction must be obeyed.

### (e) *Incumbent's other Duties*

Other duties of the incumbent, as specified in Canon C 24, include the instruction of children; the preparation and presentation to the bishop of confirmation candidates; visiting, particularly of the sick and infirm; and availability to parishioners for spiritual counsel and advice.

The incumbent is under a duty to reside in the parsonage house if there is one, but he may obtain the bishop's licence to live in another fit house, or even outside his parish. He must reside in the parish, unless so licensed, for nine months out of the twelve.

It is the duty of the incumbent to convene the annual parochial church meeting, and if he is present, he acts as chairman. He is also chairman of the parochial church council and, as such, responsible for convening its meetings. He is responsible, jointly with the churchwardens, for the disposal for pious and charitable purposes of the alms given at the Communion Service, and, jointly with the parochial church council, for the allocation of other money collected in church.

## (f) *Enforcement of Duties*

The proceedings which can be taken under the Ecclesiastical Jurisdiction Measure 1963 against an incumbent (or against any other priest or deacon holding a position involving duties) for serious, persistent or continuous neglect of duty are considered in Chapter III *ante*.

There are also certain special provisions under other statutes for the enforcement of particular duties. In particular, under the Pluralities Act 1838, if, not having the necessary licence from the bishop, an incumbent fails to reside in the parish for the required period in each year, he is liable to forfeit a proportionate part of the annual value of the benefice, and if he continues to be non-resident against the bishop's order, the profits of the benefice may be sequestrated by the bishop. Further, if such a sequestration remains in force during the incumbent's absence without leave for a whole year, the benefice becomes automatically vacant.

The Incumbents (Disability) Measure 1945 deals with cases where, through disability of mind or body or through age, an incumbent is unable to discharge adequately the duties of his benefice. The bishop may refer such a case to a Ministerial Committee with instructions to investigate and report: and the bishop's powers under the Measure will depend on the substance of the Committee's report. If the report is to the effect that the incumbent needs assistance, the bishop may, with the incumbent's consent, appoint an assistant curate to discharge certain of his duties, or the bishop may give the incumbent leave of absence up to two years and make provision for the duties during that absence. If the Committee report that the incumbent ought to resign, or if the incumbent has not consented to the appointment of an assistant curate by the bishop, the bishop may declare the benefice vacant; but in that case the Measure confers special pension rights on the incumbent.

### (g) *Avoidance of Benefice*

When an incumbent ceases to serve the duties of the cure, this is said to be an 'avoidance of the benefice'. This may occur by death, resignation, exchange, cession or deprivation, or by a declaration by the bishop under the Incumbents (Disability) Measure 1945. It also occurs if a sequestration of the profits of the benefice, consequent upon the incumbent's non-residence, continues for a full year, during the continued absence of the incumbent.

In order to effect an exchange the incumbents must obtain the consent of the respective patrons and diocesan bishops. Cession takes place when an incumbent is created a diocesan bishop, or when he is appointed to another benefice or preferment which he cannot lawfully hold with the benefice already held by him at the time of his appointment (in this connexion, the Pastoral Measure 1968 provides that, in general, no person can hold benefices in plurality except in pursuance of a pastoral scheme or order, and that no person can hold a cathedral preferment with a benefice unless the cathedral statutes so provide or allow). Deprivation takes effect where there has been simony in connexion with the presentation, institution, collation or admission to the benefice, whether the incumbent was or was not a party thereto, or where the incumbent was disqualified from holding the benefice, or by a censure of deprivation pronounced by the bishop or the court (under the Ecclesiastical Jurisdiction Measure 1963) for an offence by the incumbent.

An incumbent ceases to have any rights to the emoluments of his benefice on the date when his incumbency ceases, and these emoluments from that date become the property of his successor, when appointed, subject to the cost of providing for the performance of the duties during the vacancy. As explained in Chapter IX, a sequestration issues on the vacancy occurring, usually to the churchwardens.

When, however, an incumbent dies and there is a parsonage house attached to the benefice, his widow may continue to reside in the house for two calendar months.

## (2) THE UNBENEFICED CLERGY

Every person in holy orders who does not hold a benefice is said to be 'unbeneficed', but the great majority of these (apart from retired clergy) fall under two categories, curates-in-charge and assistant curates, and the following description applies to them. Other unbeneficed clergy do not fall within the scope of this book.

The term 'curate' means a person to whom the cure of souls is duly committed, and in a parish the person to whom the term should be applied is pre-eminently the incumbent. The popular description of an assistant clergyman licensed to a parish by the bishop as 'the curate' is erroneous. Equally misleading is it to speak of an assistant curate, informally attached by the incumbent to a chapel-of-ease, as the 'curate-in-charge'.

Sometimes it is necessary, as a temporary measure, to appoint an unbeneficed clergyman to the charge of a parish. This happens during a vacancy in the benefice, during a sequestration consequent on the incumbent's non-residence, during the permitted non-residence of the incumbent, during the suspension of an incumbent found guilty of an ecclesiastical offence, or during a suspension of presentation under section 67 of the Pastoral Measure 1968.[1] In all these cases the clergyman is called a curate-in-charge, and he performs the duties of the cure in the place of the incumbent. If any of the above circumstances arise in a parish where there is a duly licensed assistant curate he is usually, though not necessarily, appointed as curate-in-charge.

The growth of the population and its concentration in urban centres has been much more rapid than the division of the ancient parishes, and one result of this is that in places the incumbent has found himself responsible to his bishop for the spiritual welfare of many thousands of persons. In these and other circumstances he is assisted by other clergy, who have been licensed to the parish as assistant curates. The legal status of these clerks is peculiar.

An assistant curate, if not newly ordained to a parish, sometimes comes to it for a short time on trial at the invitation of the incumbent with the permission of the bishop. During this period he has no security of tenure and may be dismissed at the pleasure of the incumbent. In order to gain security, an assistant curate must be licensed to his curacy by the bishop who must be satisfied of his personal fitness. In order to be licensed he must be nomi-

[1] See p. 54 *post.*

nated by the incumbent of the parish in which he is to serve, and if he comes from another diocese he must produce to the bishop a testimonial from the bishop of the diocese in which he was last licensed, setting forth his 'honesty, ability, and conformity to the law of the church'.

The licence granted to an assistant curate is an instrument under the seal of the bishop, who thereby confers upon him a security of tenure in the curacy. The licence always states the amount of the stipend agreed upon by the incumbent and the assistant curate, for the payment of which the incumbent is responsible.[1]

Any subsequent or collateral agreement to pay or receive less than the amount specified in the licence is of no legal effect. The licence may be withdrawn at any time by the bishop after he has given the assistant curate an opportunity of being heard, and subject to a right of appeal by the assistant curate to the archbishop of the province. But the incumbent has in general no power to determine the appointment of the assistant curate after the licence has been issued, except with the bishop's consent, his powers in the matter being limited to making representations to the bishop. A parochial church council may also complain to the bishop, and the churchwardens can make a presentment on the subject to the archdeacon or the bishop at the visitation.

The assistant curate may, on the other hand, resign on giving three months' notice to the incumbent, and in practice it is usual, if any complaint is proposed to be made to higher authority, to give an assistant curate an opportunity of tendering his resignation, unless the grounds of complaint are such as to constitute a scandal.

The security of tenure referred to above is subject to the exception that a new incumbent may at any time within six months after his institution or collation dismiss an assistant curate already licensed to the parish, after giving him six weeks' notice.

On being licensed the assistant curate takes the oath of canonical obedience to the bishop, and he must on the *first* Sunday upon which he officiates in the church of the parish to which he

---

[1] In practice, the incumbent is frequently relieved of the liability in whole or in part by contributions from diocesan funds and from the parochial church council.

has been licensed 'read himself in', i.e. make the declaration of assent[1] in the presence of the congregation. In a parish containing more than one church this provision is complied with if the declaration is read in any one of the churches. It is preferable, however, that it should be read in the parish church in order that the churchwardens may certify the fact.

If any dispute arises between an incumbent and a licensed assistant curate as to the payment of the stipend or any matter connected therewith, the question is determined by the bishop, from whom there is no appeal.

Copies of all licences to assistant curates are sent to the churchwardens for safe custody in the parish chest.

## (3) MEMBERS OF TEAM AND GROUP MINISTRIES

In the context of a team ministry, the words 'rector' and 'vicar' are used in special senses quite different from their traditional meanings.

The incumbent of the benefice or benefices to which a team ministry extends is always styled 'rector'. His office may be either a perpetual or 'freehold' office (as in the case of an incumbent of an ordinary benefice) or it may be limited by the pastoral scheme establishing the team ministry to a term of years only, with security of tenure during that term.

The other members of the ministry are styled 'vicars', and the office of vicar must be limited to a specified term of years, with security of tenure during that term. Vicars are chosen by the rector and the bishop jointly. They are appointed by licence of the bishop and publicly admitted in a church in the area of the team ministry.

The rector is the leader of the team, and has a general responsibility for the cure of souls in the area. But there is power for the pastoral scheme or, subject to the scheme, for the bishop's licence appointing any vicar, to assign to such vicar a special cure of souls in respect of part of the area, or a special responsibility for a particular pastoral function, and further to provide that the special cure or responsibility shall be independent of the rector's general responsibility; and the rector's general responsibility is subject to any special cure or responsibility given to a

[1] See p. 42 *ante*.

vicar under these powers. There is also power for the scheme or the licence to assign to a vicar a general responsibility to be shared with the rector for the cure of souls in the area as a whole.

Apart from any exercise of the above-mentioned powers, a vicar, by virtue of his office but subject to his licence, has authority to perform in the area of the team ministry all such offices and services as may be performed by an incumbent.

A group ministry is an association of incumbents, whose benefices are grouped together to form the area of the ministry. Each incumbent has authority to perform, in the area of every benefice within the group, all such offices and services as may be performed by the incumbent of that benefice; and all the incumbents are under a duty to assist each other, so as to make the best possible provision for the cure of souls throughout the area of the group ministry. But each incumbent, when operating in the area of a benefice other than his own, is bound to comply with the directions of the incumbent of that other benefice.

So long as any benefice is included in a group ministry its incumbent cannot resign from the group without also resigning his benefice.

The special provisions contained in the Pastoral Measure 1968 concerning parochial church meetings and councils, and district church councils and group councils, within the areas of team and group ministries, include provisions conferring either membership of those bodies, or rights of attendance, on all the clergy participating in any such ministry. The text of the provisions in question is set out in Chapter XI.[1]

[1] See p. 124 *post*.

CHAPTER VII

## THE PATRON AND PATRONAGE

The right to present or appoint a person to a benefice is known as the right of patronage, and if the right is perpetual it is known as an advowson. The person in whom the right is vested is called the patron. The origin of ecclesiastical patronage is ancient and obscure, but it may be taken to have grown up gradually as an incident of the system by which, if a lord founded a church on his demesne, he acquired the right of patronage as the ordinary consequence.

The right of patronage is a form of property which the owner is freely entitled to deal with in his lifetime or by his will as he thinks fit, subject to the restrictions on sale which are mentioned below. But, under the Benefices Act 1898, any transfer of a right of patronage must be registered in the diocesan registry within one month from the date thereof or such extended time as the bishop may in special circumstances allow.

Where the patronage of a benefice belongs to an infant beneficially, the legal right to it is vested in trustees who make the presentation on his behalf. If and so long as a patron is a person of unsound mind the right of presentation passes to the Crown.

A Roman Catholic cannot exercise the right of presentation to a benefice, and if and so long as a patron is a Roman Catholic the right passes by certain rules to one of the universities of Oxford and Cambridge.

The patron of a benefice may be a private person, or any other person or corporation recognised by law. Thus the Queen may be patron in her capacity as a private individual, or in her capacity as supreme patron by virtue of her office, or in right of a royal duchy such as the Duchy of Lancaster; and it may be mentioned that whenever a benefice becomes vacant by the promotion of the incumbent to a bishopric, the right of presentation to the benefice for that turn passes to the Crown. Each of the diocesan bishops is the patron of many of the benefices in

51

his own diocese. Patronage is also held by the Lord Chancellor, and by universities, colleges and cathedral bodies, and it may be held by a body of trustees appointed for that special purpose.

Every diocese has a diocesan board of patronage with a mixed clerical and lay membership under the chairmanship of the bishop, which exists for the purpose of acquiring and exercising rights of patronage. But the board cannot accept a transfer of a right of patronage without the consent of the parochial church council of the parish concerned.

When a new benefice is created (by union or otherwise) under a pastoral scheme, the scheme can make whatever provision is thought fit as to the patronage thereof (though regard is to be had to the interests of former patrons whose rights have been extinguished by the scheme); if no express provision is made, the diocesan board of patronage will be the patron. When a pastoral scheme creates a team ministry, the scheme itself may designate the first 'rector'; subject to any such designation, and so long as the team ministry continues, the right of patronage will be exercised either by the bishop (if he was originally the sole patron of the benefice), or (in any other case) by the diocesan board of patronage or a specially constituted board as the scheme may provide. In the case of a group ministry, existing rights of patronage in respect of benefices included in the group are not disturbed, but so long as the group ministry continues, a patron may not exercise his right of presentation without the bishop's approval of the person presented.

If a patron neglects to present within six calendar months of the avoidance of the benefice, the right of presentation passes by lapse to the bishop of the diocese, and failing an appointment by him to the archbishop of the province, and in the last resort to the Queen. The time allowed to the bishop and the archbishop is the same as that allowed to the patron. Neglect of this kind by the patron only affects his right of presentation for that turn, and the general right of patronage remains in the patron.

Under the Benefices Act 1898 (Amendment) Measure 1923, a presentation to a benefice of which the presentee or his wife, or someone on his or her behalf, has since the passing of the Measure (on the 14th July 1924) become the patron, is void. The same Measure prohibits any sale of a right of patronage after the next two vacancies in the benefice subsequent to the passing of the Measure. As a result of this prohibition and the subsequent passage of time, the rights of patronage in respect of all but a very small minority of the benefices in the country are by now unsaleable. It should also be mentioned that new rights of patronage created under the Pastoral Measure 1968 or the enactments which preceded it are likewise, by express provision, unsaleable.

By virtue of the Benefices (Transfer of Rights of Patronage) Measure 1930, notice of a proposed transfer of a right of patronage must be given by the bishop to the churchwardens and the secretary of the parochial church council of the parish concerned. Any objections to the proposal may be sent to the bishop within fourteen days, and such objections must then be sent by the bishop to the patron. If the patron is the bishop himself, he must, if the council so resolve and communicate their resolution to him within twenty-one days, confer with the council on the subject of the proposed transfer.

Further provisions relating to the parochial church council are contained in the Benefices (Exercise of Rights of Presentation) Measure 1931. When a vacancy in a benefice is impending, the bishop must give notice thereof to the patron and to the council, and the latter may then make written representations to the patron as to the needs and traditions of the parish, without, however, mentioning the name of any particular clerk.

The council may also, within thirty days after notice of a vacancy or impending vacancy, pass a resolution that section 3 of the Measure is to have effect, and the resolution must be communicated to the bishop and to the patron. In such a case the patron may present to the benefice after consulting with, and obtaining the consent of, the churchwardens as representing the council. If within sixty days of the original notification of vacancy such consent is not given or a conference has not taken place for some reason other than the neglect or refusal of the patron, the patron may present after obtaining the bishop's approval of the clerk presented. The bishop may, before giving or withholding his approval, and shall if the patron or council require, consult the body of advisers set up by section 4 of the Measure. If the bishop finally withholds his approval, the patron may appeal to the archbishop (if the archbishop himself is the diocesan, the appeal lies to the other archbishop). If the bishop is himself the patron, he must consult the churchwardens as representing the council, and he may, and if required by them shall, consult the body of advisers, before collating a clerk to the benefice.

The body of advisers consists of three clergymen elected by the house of clergy of the diocesan synod, four laymen elected by the house of laity of that synod, and the archdeacon, who is also the chairman.

The Measure does not affect the rights as patron of the Crown, the Duchy of Lancaster, the Duchy of Cornwall or Greenwich Hospital.

The Benefices (Purchase of Rights of Patronage) Measure 1933 conferred on a parochial church council certain rights of compulsory purchase of the patronage of a benefice where a transfer of the patronage was registered at any time after 14th July 1924, and at the date of such registration two vacancies in the benefice had not occurred since that date. Owing to the passage of time, there can by now remain only a few benefices in respect of which the rights conferred by this Measure can possibly arise in practice.

Under Section 67 of the Pastoral Measure 1968, the bishop may, in the case of a vacant benefice or one which is shortly to become vacant, with the consent of the pastoral committee and after consultation with the patron and with the parochial church council concerned, give notice that, for a period of not more than five years, the patron is not to exercise his right of presentation without the consent of the pastoral committee and the bishop. The period of suspension may thereafter be extended an indefinite number of times, by notice served by the bishop, with the same consent and after the same consultation, from time to time before each current period of suspension expires; but the period is not to be extended for more than five years by any one such notice.

During any period of suspension, there is a sequestration of the profits of the benefice, out of which provision is made for the performance of the duties of the cure.

# CHAPTER VIII

## THE OFFICE OF CHURCHWARDEN

The office of churchwarden is a venerable one, which had already emerged into legal recognition by the thirteenth century. Two centuries later the churchwardens were chosen annually in parish meeting, all adult parishioners having a voice in the election. Once elected, the churchwardens normally transacted all parish business during their year of office. They had, in fact, a two-fold significance; they were both guardians of the parochial morals and trustees of the Church's goods.

The functions of churchwardens at the present time are dealt with in the next chapter of this book. This present chapter is concerned with their qualification and manner of appointment, and with the modes whereby the office of churchwarden may be vacated. The law on these subjects is now contained almost entirely in the Churchwardens (Appointment and Resignation) Measure 1964, as amended in some respects by the Synodical Government Measure 1969. The Measure of 1964 is, to a large extent, a re-statement in statutory form of the pre-existing law, but it has introduced some changes, the more important of which are mentioned in the notes to the Measure below.

## CHURCHWARDENS (APPOINTMENT AND RESIGNATION) MEASURE 1964 (AS AMENDED), WITH NOTES

A MEASURE passed by the National Assembly of the Church of England to regulate the number and qualifications of, and the time and manner of choosing, churchwardens of parishes; to regulate their admission to office; to provide for the resignation of churchwardens and for their vacating their offices in certain events; to regulate the qualifications of churchwardens of Guild Churches in the City of London; and for purposes connected therewith.                    [27th February 1964]

Number and qualifications of church-wardens.

**1.** (1) Subject to the provisions of this Measure there shall be two churchwardens of every parish.[1]

(2) The churchwardens of every parish shall be chosen from persons who are resident in the parish or whose names are on the church electoral roll of the parish.

(3) Such persons shall be actual communicant members of the Church of England except where the bishop shall otherwise permit and of twenty-one years of age and upwards.[2]

(4) No person shall be chosen as a churchwarden unless he has signified his consent to serve.[3]

Time and manner of choosing church-wardens.

**2.** (1) The churchwardens of a parish shall be chosen annually not later than the 30th April in each year.[4]

(2) Subject to the provisions of this Measure the church-wardens of a parish shall be chosen by the joint consent of the minister of the parish and a meeting of the parishioners if it may be; such joint consent shall be deemed to have been signified:—

(*a*) if any motion stating the names of the persons to be chosen as churchwardens or the name of either of them

---

[1] Exceptionally, there may be a different number by custom; see section 12 (2) below. There is now another exception under the Pastoral Measure 1968: where a pastoral scheme designates two or more parish churches in a single parish (see p. 33 *ante*), two churchwardens are appointed for each of those churches, and the Churchwardens (Appointment and Resignation) Measure 1964 applies separately to each pair of churchwardens; but all the churchwardens are churchwardens of the whole parish, except so far as they may arrange to perform separate duties in relation to the several parish churches.

[2] Previously to the Measure, membership of the Church of England was an essential qualification in new but not in ancient parishes. The requirement of being an 'actual communicant' is entirely new. The qualifying age is still twenty-one, notwithstanding that eighteen is now 'full age' under the general law.

[3] Previously, in ancient parishes, every householder could be made to serve, except for certain classes of persons who were exempted or disqualified.

[4] Printed as amended by the Synodical Government Measure 1969. The original requirement as to time was 'not later in the year than during the week following Easter week'. In practice, the meeting is usually held on the same day as and immediately before the annual parochial church meeting (see p. 87 *post*).

shall be declared by the person presiding over the meeting to have been carried; and

(b) if in respect of any such motion the minister shall have announced his consent to the choice of the person or persons named therein either before the putting of the motion to the meeting or immediately upon the declaration of the result thereof:

Provided that no person shall be deemed to have been chosen as a churchwarden under the provisions of this subsection unless both churchwardens have been so chosen.[1]

(3) If the minister of the parish and the meeting of the parishioners cannot agree on the choice of both church-wardens by joint consent as provided in the foregoing subsection or if after due opportunity has been given no motions or insufficient motions have been moved in accordance with the provisions of that subsection then one churchwarden shall be appointed by the minister and the other shall then be elected by the meeting of the parishioners.

(4) During any period when there is no minister both the churchwardens shall be elected by the meeting of the parishioners.

(5) A person may be chosen to fill a casual vacancy among the churchwardens at any time.

(6) Any person chosen to fill a casual vacancy shall be chosen in the same manner as was the churchwarden in whose place he is appointed.[2]

---

[1] This sub-section reproduces in substance the rule previously obtaining. It is now, as it has always been, incorrect, as is so often the practice, for the incumbent to choose one churchwarden and the parishioners the other, without first attempting to agree to the choice of both.

[2] It is conceived that if the churchwarden whose place has to be filled was himself chosen by agreement between minister and parishioners, but they cannot agree on any person to fill the casual vacancy, the vacancy must remain unfilled until the next annual meeting.

E

**Meeting of the parishioners.**

**3.** (1) A joint meeting of:—

(a) the persons whose names are entered on the church electoral roll of the parish; and

(b) the persons resident in the parish whose names are entered on a register of local government electors by reason of such residence:

shall be deemed to be a meeting of the parishioners for the purposes of this Measure.

(2) The meeting of the parishioners shall be convened by the minister or the churchwardens of the parish by a notice signed by the minister or a churchwarden.

(3) The notice shall state the place, day and hour at which the meeting of the parishioners is to be held.

(4) The notice shall be affixed on or near to the principal door of the parish church and of every other building licensed for public worship in the parish for a period including the last two Sundays before the meeting.

(5) The minister, if present, or, if he is not present, a chairman chosen by the meeting of the parishioners, shall preside thereat.

(6) In case of an equal division of votes the chairman of the meeting of the parishioners shall have a casting vote.[1]

(7) The meeting of the parishioners shall have power to adjourn, and to determine its own rules of procedure.

(8) A person appointed by the meeting of the parishioners shall act as clerk of the meeting and shall record the minutes thereof.

**4, 5 and 6. . . .**[2]

**Admission of churchwardens.**

**7.** (1) At a time and place to be appointed by the ordinary each person chosen for the office of churchwarden shall

---

[1] The Synodical Government Measure 1969 provides that this sub-section shall not apply to elections of churchwardens. It accordingly now only applies to votes on procedural matters (e.g. a proposal to adjourn).

[2] Sections 4, 5 and 6, relating to the procedure applicable to elections, were repealed by the Synodical Government Measure 1969. These matters are now dealt with by rules 10 and 11 of the Church Representation Rules set out in Schedule 3 to that Measure (see p. 91 *post*).

appear before the ordinary, or his substitute duly appointed, and be admitted to the office of churchwarden after subscribing the declaration that he will faithfully and diligently perform the duties of his office, and making the same in the presence of the ordinary or his substitute. No person chosen for the office of churchwarden shall become churchwarden until such time as he shall have been admitted to office in accordance with the provisions of this section.[1]

(2) Subject to the provisions of this Measure the churchwardens so chosen and admitted as aforesaid shall continue in their office until they, or others as their successors, be admitted in like manner before the ordinary.

**8.** (1) If a churchwarden wishes to resign his office he may, with the consent in writing of the minister and any other churchwarden of the parish, resign his office by an instrument in writing addressed to the bishop, and if the bishop accepts his resignation his office shall forthwith be vacated.

Resignation of churchwardens.

(2) Subject to the provisions of this section a churchwarden shall not be entitled to resign his office.[2]

**9.** The office of churchwarden shall be vacated if the churchwarden is not resident in the parish and if his name is not on the church electoral roll of the parish.[3]

Vacation of office.

---

[1] The admission of churchwardens, after subscribing the declaration referred to in this sub-section, ordinarily takes place at the annual 'visitation'. It is usual for a bishop to 'visit' his diocese from time to time, and in those years when he does not do so a visitation is held, on his behalf, by the archdeacon in each archdeaconry. In the case of an episcopal visitation the admission takes place before the bishop or his chancellor or surrogate. In other years it is performed by the archdeacon or his official. It is open to any person to allege that some cause exists why the persons claiming admission should not be admitted to office; and the bishop or archdeacon, as the case may be, may make inquiries before admitting a person even if no such cause is alleged. A fee of one guinea, for which the churchwardens are personally liable, is charged for each parish (see p. 115 *post*). If for any reason the bishop or archdeacon refuses to admit a person to the office of churchwarden the remedy is by proceedings in the High Court of Justice.
[2] Previously to the Measure, the question whether a churchwarden could validly resign was doubtful.
[3] This is a new provision.

**Guild
Churches.**

**10.** (1) In the case of every church in the City of London designated and established as a Guild Church under the City of London (Guild Churches) Acts, 1952 and 1960, the churchwardens shall, notwithstanding anything to the contrary contained in those Acts, be actual communicant members of the Church of England except where the bishop shall otherwise permit.

(2) Subject to the provisions of subsection (1) of this section, nothing in this Measure shall apply to the churchwardens of any church designated and established as a Guild Church under the City of London (Guild Churches) Acts 1952 and 1960.[1]

**Special
provisions.**

**11.** (1) In the carrying out of this Measure in any diocese the bishop of such diocese shall have power:—

(*a*) to make provision for any matter not herein provided for;

(*b*) to appoint a person to do any act in respect of which there has been any neglect or default on the part of any person or body charged with any duty under this Measure;

(*c*) so far as may be necessary for the purpose of giving effect to the intentions of this Measure, to extend or alter the time for holding any meeting or election or to modify the procedure laid down by this Measure in connection therewith;

(*d*) in any case in which there has been no valid choice to direct a fresh choice to be made, and to give such directions in connection therewith as he may think necessary; and

(*e*) in any case in which any difficulty arises, to give any directions which he may consider expedient for the purpose of removing the difficulty.

(2) The powers of the bishop under this section shall not

[1] As to guild churches generally, see p. 38 *ante*. Under the Act of 1952, the churchwardens of a guild church (two in number) are chosen by the vicar and members of the guild church electoral roll at an annual guild church meeting held in each year before Low Sunday. Eligible candidates are persons who are either on the guild church electoral roll, or eligible to be churchwardens of some parish in the City of London.

enable him to validate anything that was invalid at the
time it was done.

(3) . . .[1]

(4) During a vacancy in a diocesan see the powers by
this section conferred upon a bishop of the diocese shall
be exercisable by the guardian of the spiritualities.[2]

**12.** (1) Subject to the provisions of section ten of this **Savings**
Measure, nothing in this Measure shall be deemed to
amend, repeal or affect any local act or any scheme made
under any enactment affecting the churchwardens of a
parish:

Provided that for the purposes of this Measure the
Parish of Manchester Division Act, 1850, shall be deemed
to be a general act.

(2) In the case of any parish where there is an existing
custom which regulates the number of churchwardens or
the manner in which the churchwardens are chosen,
nothing in this Measure shall affect that custom:[3]

Provided that in the case of any parish where in accordance with that custom any churchwarden is chosen by the
vestry of that parish either alone or jointly with any other
person or persons that churchwarden shall be chosen by
the meeting of the parishioners, either alone or jointly with
the other person or persons, as the case may be.

(3) Nothing in this Measure shall affect a churchwarden
in office before the passing of this Measure during the
period for which he was chosen.

(4) Nothing in this Measure shall be deemed to authorise
the choice of any person as churchwarden who under the

---

[1] This sub-section, which related to the form of voting paper to be
used at elections, was repealed by the Synodical Government
Measure 1969. See now the Church Representation Rules, rules 10
and 11 (p. 91 *post*).

[2] See p. 1 *ante*.

[3] Instances of local customs are numerous. There can be a valid
custom whereby there may be only one churchwarden, or three or
more churchwardens, for a parish, or whereby churchwardens are
elected for separate parts of the parish. In most ancient parishes in
the City of London, there is a custom whereby both churchwardens
are chosen by the parishioners.

existing law is disqualified from being chosen for that office.[1]

**Interpretation.** **13.** In this Measure, except in so far as the context otherwise requires:—

"existing custom" means a custom existing at the commencement of this Measure which has continued for a period including the last forty years before its commencement.[2]

"Rules for the Representation of the Laity" means the Rules for the Representation of the Laity[3] contained in the Schedule to the Representation of the Laity Measure, 1956;

"actual communicant member", "minister", "parish" and "public worship" have the same meanings respectively as those assigned to those expressions in Rule 1 of the Rules for the Representation of the Laity.[3]

**14 . . .**[4]

**Short title, extent and commencement.** **15.** (1) This Measure may be cited as the Churchwardens (Appointment and Resignation) Measure, 1964.

(2) This Measure shall extend to the whole of the provinces of Canterbury and York except for the Channel Islands and the Isle of Man:

Provided that—

(a) this Measure may be applied to the Channel Islands as defined in the Channel Islands (Church Legislation)

[1] Aliens, also persons who have been convicted of felony, perjury, or fraud, are amongst those who are disqualified.

[2] i.e. the last forty years before 1st January 1965: see section 15 (3). The forty years' qualification period was presumably imposed in order to prevent the continuation or revival of doubtful or half-forgotten customs.

[3] The Rules for the Representation of the Laity have been replaced by the Church Representation Rules (Synodical Government Measure 1969, Schedule 3). The relevant definitions are now contained in Rule 44 of the last-mentioned Rules (p. 102 *post*).

[4] Section 14 merely repealed certain previous enactments and it is unnecessary to reproduce it here.

Measures, 1931 and 1957, or either of them in accordance with those Measures;

(*b*) if an Act of Tynwald so provides this Measure shall extend to the Isle of Man subject to such modifications, if any, as may be specified in such Act of Tynwald.

(3) This Measure shall come into force on the first day of January next after the date on which it receives the Royal Assent.

# CHAPTER IX

# THE FUNCTION OF CHURCHWARDENS

## (1) CHURCHWARDENS AND CHAPELWARDENS

In this chapter it is proposed to consider the functions of churchwardens after their admission to office. These functions extend to every consecrated church and chapel within the parish. While it is usual to have wardens in a chapel-of-ease, these (unless appointed in accordance with one or other of the statutory provisions mentioned below) do not as such have any legal status, nor can they act as *church*wardens unless the churchwardens of the parish give them the authority to do so; and even in that case they act only as the agents of the churchwardens. It is desirable, therefore, that such wardens should be appointed as sidesmen of the parish church, by which means they may be given a legal status as officers of the parish, with the duty of assisting the churchwardens in the exercise of their office.

Under the Pastoral Measure 1968, in the case of a team ministry established by a pastoral scheme, provision can be made for the election, by the annual parochial church meeting of any parish comprised within the area of the scheme, of a 'district church council' and 'deputy churchwardens' for any district in the parish which contains a church or place of worship; and for assigning to the deputy churchwardens any of the functions of the churchwardens of the parish, being functions relating to that church or place of worship or district. The text of the relevant provision is set out in full in Chapter XI of this book.[1] And under rule 16 (4) of the Church Representation Rules (forming

[1] See p. 123 *post.*

Schedule 3 to the Synodical Government Measure 1969)[1], a procedure is laid down which, if it is followed, enables a 'district church council' to be constituted, and 'deputy churchwardens' to be elected or chosen, for any church or place of worship situated within a parish which is not itself the parish church.

Reference may also here be made to the case of a parish which by virtue of a pastoral scheme has two or more parish churches, each with its set of two churchwardens. Such churchwardens may, if they think fit, arrange to perform separate duties in relation to the several parish churches.[2]

It may be mentioned in passing that if the 'wardens' of a chapel-of-ease undertake the care of the funds of the congregation, or of moneys raised by the congregation for a particular purpose such as the maintenance of the fabric, they thereby constitute themselves trustees of the funds or moneys in question, and will be answerable for their proper expenditure. But they are not personally liable on a contract unless they bind themselves expressly.

## (2) POWERS AND DUTIES

### (a) *As to Church, Churchyard and Contents of Church*

The incumbent is the person in whom the freehold of church and churchyard is vested. But possession of both is vested in the incumbent and churchwardens jointly, and if any person claims to enter a church for any purpose other than assisting at a service, the incumbent and churchwardens together have the right to prevent him.

While the incumbent has the custody of the key of the church, the churchwardens have the right of access to the church for the proper discharge of their duties.

All the movable furniture and ornaments of the church are in the legal ownership of the churchwardens, but the clergy must be allowed any use of these objects which is necessary for their ministrations. The churchwardens must not remove furnishings or ornaments or introduce new ones without a faculty or an archdeacon's certificate[3] unless such action amounts merely to

[1] See p. 95 *post* for the text of this provision.
[2] See p. 56 *ante*.
[3] See Chapter IV *ante*.

replacing any article which is worn out, and even this should only be done in consultation with the incumbent. If any article is stolen, the churchwardens may take all the steps necessary for its recovery and for the prosecution of the thief.

The care, maintenance, preservation and insurance of the fabric of the church, and of the goods and ornaments thereof, and the repair of the churchyard fence and other structures, are, under the modern law, the responsibility of the parochial church council and not of the churchwardens as such.

### (b) *Maintenance of Order*

It is the duty of churchwardens to maintain order in the church and churchyard, especially during divine service. They may remove persons who disturb the performance of the service, or who show that they intend to do so. Thus, it has been held that a churchwarden could properly remove a man's hat if he refused to remove it during divine service after being requested to do so.

It is a criminal offence at common law to strike any person in a church or churchyard. And under the Brawling in Churches Act 1860, riotous, violent, or indecent behaviour in any church, churchyard or burial ground, is an offence punishable by fine or imprisonment; so also is the disturbance of a duly authorised preacher, or of any clergyman celebrating any sacrament or divine service. Any person offending under this Act may be arrested by any constable or churchwarden of the parish or place.

These provisions apply to clergy and laity alike. It is to be observed, however, that the churchwardens cannot interfere with the conduct of the services by the minister unless his behaviour is such as to bring him within the purview of the Act. In any other case they have no remedy except by way of complaint to the bishop.

### (c) *Allocation of Seats*

Churchwardens are entrusted with the duty of providing seats for the parishioners. In this capacity they act as the officers of the bishop, who at common law had the right of disposal of the seats. Their rights and duties in this respect may be limited by some over-riding right of a private person, e.g. when a particular pew is attached to an estate by prescription. Subject, however, to any such rights as these, and subject also, in a church where there are pew-rents, to the rights of the pew-holders, the churchwardens may direct persons where to sit, and where not to sit, and may do this beforehand or for a particular service or for an indefinite period. But they cannot legally give the right to a particular seat for all time, because to do so would divest themselves or their successors of the liberty to rearrange the seating accommodation at a future time. Seats can legally be assigned only to parishioners, and before dispossessing a parishioner of a seat normally occupied by him, the churchwardens would be well advised to give him notice of their intention, in order that he may show cause why he should not be so dispossessed.

This control of the seating accommodation belongs to the churchwardens in the interests of good order. They cannot exclude an orderly person on the ground that the church is full if he can stand in such a part of the church as will not interfere with the conduct of the service. It is illegal to demand payment, by way of rent or otherwise, for the exclusive use of a seat, unless there is express statutory permission applicable to the church in question. If a parishioner intrudes himself into a seat contrary to the directions of the churchwardens, they may remove him, provided that they do not use unnecessary force or cause a scandal by disturbing the worship of the church.

## (d) *Alms and Collections*

The matter of the disposal of money collected in church is an important one upon which misunderstanding exists. In the first place a distinction must be made between the alms given at the Communion Service and collections given at other times. The use of the word 'offertory' to denote a collection is incorrect and misleading. Strictly the offertory is merely a stage in the Communion Service during which alms may be collected.

The churchwardens are entrusted with the collection of the Communion alms. Their disposal, by the authority of a rubric in the Prayer Book which is confirmed by section 7 of the Parochial Church Council (Powers) Measure 1956,[1] rests with the minister and churchwardens for such pious and charitable

[1] See pp. 120, 121 *post*.

uses as they think fit, and if they fail to agree, as the bishop appoints.

As regards collections taken in church otherwise than at Communion Services, the power of allocation rests, under section 7 of the Parochial Church Council (Powers) Measure 1956, with the incumbent and the parochial church council; and the churchwardens as such are not concerned. Presumably the churchwardens' duties with respect to these collections are confined to receiving the money, and holding it (until handed over to the treasurer or other authorised person) as agents for the incumbent and the council.

### (e) *Vacancy of Benefice*

When a vacancy occurs in a benefice the churchwardens are usually (even though not necessarily) appointed sequestrators. Some description of the process of sequestration may therefore not be considered out of place here. This process is issued by the bishop, and under it the income is ordered to be taken by the sequestrators and applied by them in manner required by the circumstances of the case. It may be issued if the incumbent becomes of unsound mind, or for the recovery of a judgment debt from him or on his bankruptcy, and in certain other cases,[1] as well as when a benefice becomes vacant.

In the case of a vacancy the persons to whom the warrant of sequestration is issued receive the profits, and pay out of them the cost of serving the cure during the vacancy. They may also, in certain circumstances, incur other expenses. They account for these to the new incumbent, and pay him any balance which they have in hand, or, on the other hand, recover from him any debit balance.

When churchwardens are appointed as sequestrators they act in the sequestration not as churchwardens but as sequestrators. The parochial church council has no status in the matter.

Immediately a benefice becomes vacant from any cause other than the resignation of the incumbent, the churchwardens should notify the bishop and the patron. The bishop will then probably cause the sequestration warrant to be issued, and thereupon the benefice, with the exception of the parsonage house, passes into

[1] For other examples, see pp. 45 and 54 *ante*.

possession of the bishop and of the sequestrators as his agents. The latter may then, by virtue of the Sequestration Act 1849, take any necessary proceedings in their own names to recover rents or other debts due to the benefice, but this does not extend to arrears of rents which have accrued prior to the sequestration. If the incumbent dies while in occupation of the parsonage house his widow is entitled to occupy the house for two months from his death.

If there is in the parish a licensed assistant curate at the time when the vacancy occurs, he continues in office and his stipend is paid by the sequestrators. If there is no assistant curate, or if he is unable by himself to perform all the duties of the cure, the bishop may appoint and licence one or more other curates to minister in the parish during the vacancy, and these are paid by the sequestrators, who may themselves employ clergy for the purpose if the bishop does not act. The bishop may assign to any curate or curates appointed to perform the duties a stipend or stipends not exceeding in the aggregate the net annual income of the benefice.

It has been held that the custody of the register books of the church during a vacancy in the benefice rests with the churchwardens.

Before a successor is appointed, the patron, if not himself the bishop, notifies to the bishop the name of the person whom he intends to present. In certain cases the patronage is vested in the parochial church council, and the election is then conducted by the churchwardens.

Before proceeding to institute or collate the successor, the bishop must send to the churchwardens by registered post a notice of his intention, together with particulars of the ecclesiastical preferments previously held by the clergyman in question, and a direction that the notice is to be fixed on the church door or notice-board for not less than one month, and then to be returned to the bishop with the churchwardens' certificate that the direction has been complied with.

### (f) *Churchwardens as Bishops' Officers*

The churchwardens are the officers of the bishop, and it is their duty, on the bishop's or archdeacon's visitation at the end of their year of office, to answer such questions as may be put to them about the state of the parish and to report whatever may be amiss. They should also at any other time report to the bishop any irregularity or failure of duty of which he ought to be informed.

### (3) ACTIONS BY AND AGAINST CHURCHWARDENS

Apart from any special statutory enactments, churchwardens are not a 'corporation' in the legal sense of having a corporate and continuous existence regardless of changes in the identity of the individual holders of the office; but they have certain attributes of a corporation. Thus they may hold church property, other than land, in perpetual succession, and in the City of London, they may hold land to the same purpose. In relation to any property so held, they can bring an action in their own names in respect of a matter which arose during the period of office of their predecessors, but they cannot be sued in respect of such a matter. Both churchwardens must concur in and be parties to the taking of legal proceedings.

Under modern law, contracts in relation to such matters as the supply of articles for use in the church, or repairs and additions to the fabric and other church property, are properly entered into, not by the churchwardens, but by the parochial church council. The council, therefore, is the proper body to sue or be sued on any such contracts.

# CHAPTER X

## OTHER LAY OFFICERS

**(1) Parish Clerk and Sexton—(2) Organist—(3) Verger—(4) Sidesmen—(5) Readers—(6) Deaconesses—(7) Women Workers.**

### (1) PARISH CLERK AND SEXTON

By Section 7 (iii) of the Parochial Church Council (Powers) Measure 1956, replacing Section 6 (iii) of the Parochial Church Council (Powers) Measure 1921, the power to appoint and dismiss the parish clerk and sexton, or any person performing or assisting to perform the duties of parish clerk or sexton, and to determine their salaries and the conditions of the tenure of their offices or of their employment, is vested jointly in the parochial church council and the incumbent.

This provision is subject to the rights of any persons holding those offices on the 1st July 1921 (being the date on which the Measure of 1921 came into force). At that time both offices were frequently offices of freehold, or otherwise held with some security of tenure. But by now there can only be very few holders of either office whose appointments date back so far.

In parishes where they are employed, parish clerks are entitled to fees on marriages and burials, and sextons to fees on burials, the respective amounts of which are now fixed by the Church Commissioners under the authority of the Ecclesiastical Fees Measure 1962; and they can sue the incumbent or the church-wardens for the recovery of such fees. In addition to fees, a parish clerk or sexton is entitled to such additional remuneration (if any) as may have been agreed under the terms of his employment.

### (2) ORGANIST

An organist may be appointed by the incumbent alone, but the only satisfactory procedure is for him to be appointed by the incumbent with the concurrence of the parochial church council,

71

so that the council can undertake responsibility for his salary. It is desirable that the terms of the appointment should be embodied in a written agreement. The office of organist is not known to the common law and an organist as such has no legal status.

The organist, when appointed, is under the control of the incumbent, who is responsible for the music in church as part of the service, and may give directions as to the playing of the organ in the same way as he may with regard to the singing.

### (3) VERGER

The strict meaning of the title of verger is the official who carries a 'verge' or mace before a dignitary. In common usage the term denotes the official who takes care of the interior of the fabric of a church. He is the servant of the persons employing him, who should be the parochial church council. It is desirable that there should be a written contract containing the terms of the employment and the conditions on which it may be terminated by either side. The liability in case of an accident to the verger arising out of, or in the course of, his employment should be covered by insurance.

### (4) SIDESMEN

The annual parochial church meeting of a parish may (but is not obliged to) elect any number of sidesmen for the forthcoming year. The only qualification for a sidesman is that he should be on the electoral roll of the parish. The duty of sidesmen, as stated in Canon E2, is to promote the cause of true religion in the parish and to assist the churchwardens in the discharge of their duties in maintaining order and decency in the church and churchyard, and especially during the time of divine service.

The practice of 'admitting' sidesmen at the same time as the churchwardens are admitted at the annual visitation has tended in recent years to fall into disuse, but is still observed in some places.

### (5) READERS

Readers (often called 'lay readers') are lay officers of the Church whose functions include general pastoral and educational work, and in particular, as regards divine service, officiating at Morning and Evening Prayer (omitting the Absolution), the publication of banns of marriage, the reading of the lessons, and preaching (see Canon E4).

Under Canon B12, and section 2 of the Prayer Book (Further Provisions) Measure 1968, a layman may be specially authorised by the bishop, acting under such regulations as the Convocations (now the General Synod) may make from time to time, to distribute the sacrament of the Lord's Supper to the people. In practice a reader is frequently authorised under this power to administer the chalice at Holy Communion.

The use made by the Church of readers has considerably increased in recent years. They usually give their services voluntarily, but it is possible for a reader to be employed in a parish at a stipend.

Any person of either sex who is baptised and confirmed, and a regular communicant of the Church of England, is qualified to become a reader; but a candidate for the office must first undergo an examination of his knowledge and competence. A new reader, before being admitted to office, makes a declaration of assent to the Thirty-nine Articles and the Prayer Book, and that he will give due obedience to the bishop; he is then admitted by the bishop delivering to him the New Testament.

An admitted reader may not exercise his office in any diocese (except temporarily, with the bishop's written permission) unless he has been licensed to do so by the bishop of that diocese. Such licence may be revoked by the bishop at any time.

A register of admitted and licensed readers is kept in each diocese.

## (6) DEACONESSES

The order of deaconesses is an order of women whose functions are pastoral care and instruction, particularly of women, young people and children. It is described in Canon D1 as 'the one order of ministry in the Church of England to which women are admitted by prayer and the laying on of hands by the bishop'; but it is not one of the 'holy orders' of the Church, and deaconesses are members of the laity for all purposes. They are normally

F

employed in parochial work on a stipendiary basis. With the bishop's permission, and at the incumbent's invitation, they may in any church or chapel read Morning and Evening Prayer and the Litany (except the portions reserved to a priest) and lead in prayer; and also instruct and preach except at the Communion Service.[1]

A candidate for admission must be at least twenty-five years old, baptised, confirmed and a regular communicant of the Church of England; and she must undergo an examination of her religious knowledge. Before admission, she makes a declaration of assent to the Thirty-nine Articles and the Prayer Book, and swears an oath of obedience to the bishop.

A deaconess may not exercise her office in any diocese (except temporarily with the bishop's written permission) unless she has been licensed to do so by the bishop of that diocese.

A register of admitted and licensed deaconesses is kept in each diocese.

## (7) WOMEN WORKERS

Women workers commissioned by the bishop are employed in some parishes on a stipendiary basis. Before commissioning a woman worker, the bishop must be satisfied that she is baptised, confirmed and a regular communicant of the Church of England, and that she possesses the necessary qualifications for the work.

A commissioned woman worker may not serve as such in any diocese (except temporarily, with the bishop's written permission) unless she has been licensed to do so by the bishop of that diocese.

Every woman worker, before being commissioned or licensed, must make a declaration of assent to the Prayer Book, and that she will give due obedience to the bishop.

A register of commissioned and licensed women workers is kept in every diocese.

[1] A proposed new canon, which would considerably widen the powers of a deaconess, has been given general approval by the General Synod, but has not as yet, at the time of writing, been finally passed as a canon.

# CHAPTER XI

# PAROCHIAL CHURCH MEETINGS AND COUNCILS

**(1) Introduction—(2) The Church Representation Rules (so far as relating to Parochial Church Meetings and Councils) with Notes—(3) The Parochial Church Council (Powers) Measure 1956 (as Amended) with Notes—(4) Provisions of Pastoral Measure 1968 relating to Parochial Church Meetings and Councils in Special Cases, with Notes.**

## (1) INTRODUCTION

Previously to the Church of England Assembly (Powers) Act 1919,[1] the administration and finances of a parish were, in law, almost exclusively the prerogative of the incumbent and church-wardens. The general body of parishioners had little or no say in these matters, except in so far as they took part in the annual appointment of churchwardens. It is true that parochial church councils had been set up in most urban parishes, but they existed at the will of the incumbent and had no powers except such as he might delegate to them. Their existence was, however, some evidence both of the wishes of the laity to take a larger share of the burdens of parochial administration, and of the desire of the clergy to allow to the laity as a whole a voice in the affairs of the parish.

Parochial church councils were given a legal status for the first time by the Act of 1919, and by the Parochial Church Council (Powers) Measure 1921, which was one of the first measures to be passed under the powers conferred by the Act. Rules as to the composition of parochial church councils, and as to the procedure in relation to meetings, were set out in a Schedule to the 'Constitution' of the Church Assembly appended to the Act, whilst the Measure defined the functions and powers of such councils.

At the present time, the composition and procedure of parochial church councils are regulated by the Church Representation Rules which constitute Schedule 3 to the Synodical Government

[1] See p. 5 *ante*.

Measure 1969, whilst their functions and powers are contained in the Parochial Church Council (Powers) Measure 1956, as amended by the Measure of 1969. But in addition to the functions conferred by the Measure of 1956, parochial church councils also have a number of particular functions conferred by various other provisions, some of which are mentioned below.

The text of such parts of the Church Representation Rules as are relevant to parochial church councils, and the whole of the Parochial Church Council (Powers) Measure 1956 (as amended), are set out in the pages which follow. But first, it may be of assistance to state briefly their general effect and the extent of the powers given to the laity in a parish.

The basis of the scheme is the electoral roll. This is a roll of persons who are qualified electors in a parish. They are lay persons of seventeen years of age or upwards, who are baptised and are members either of the Church of England, or of some other Church of the Anglican Communion, or of an overseas Church in communion with the Church of England, and who are not members of any other religious body which is not in communion with the Church of England. They must also sign the form of application set out in an appendix to the Church Representation Rules. A person cannot be a qualified elector unless he resides in the parish, or is entered on the electoral roll as a non-resident elector, and he cannot in any case be a qualified elector in more than two parishes at one time.[1]

A non-resident elector, in addition to the qualifications other than residence required of electors who are resident in the parish, must for six months preceding the date of enrolment have habitually attended public worship in the parish on whose roll he seeks to be entered.

There is provision in the Rules for an annual revision of the electoral roll; also for the preparation of an entirely new roll in the year 1972, and thereafter in every succeeding sixth year.

It may be observed in passing that the electoral roll is of importance not only as being the nominal roll of electors to the parochial church council, but also as the foundation underlying the whole scheme of lay representation from the deanery upwards. As has already been explained in Chapter II, it is the electors entered on the roll of each parish who elect parochial

[1] See further as to this, p. 81 *post*.

representatives to the house of laity of the deanery synod; again, it is the members of that house who elect deanery representatives to the house of laity of the diocesan synod; and yet again, it is the members of the houses of laity of the deanery synods in a diocese who elect the diocesan representatives to the House of Laity of the General Synod. Thus it is broadly true to say that the lay representatives of all the dioceses on the General Synod are the indirectly elected representatives of all the persons whose names are entered on the electoral rolls of all the parishes throughout the country. Nor is this all, since it is also the fact that the aggregate number of persons whose names are on the relevant electoral roll or rolls is a principal factor in determining (i) the number of lay representatives of a parish on the deanery synod, (ii) the number of lay representatives of a deanery on the diocesan synod, and (iii) the number of lay representatives of a diocese on the General Synod.[1] If, therefore, the system of lay representation is to be efficient and genuinely 'representative', it is vital that the electoral rolls in all the parishes should be kept accurately, and should be up-to-date.

The Rules provide for the holding, not later than the 30th April in each year, of an 'annual parochial church meeting' in which all those whose names are on the electoral roll of the parish are entitled to take part. This meeting elects lay members of the parochial church council; persons so elected must themselves be on the electoral roll of the parish and, as an additional qualification, they are required to be actual communicants. Other business which may be conducted at the same meeting consists of (i) the election (triennially) of lay representatives to the deanery synod, (ii) the election of sidesmen, (iii) the receiving of parochial and other reports, and (iv) the general discussion of church and parochial affairs. It is usual for this meeting to be held on the same day as and immediately after the 'meeting of the parishioners' for the appointment of churchwardens.

The incumbent or curate-in-charge of a parish is an *ex-officio* member and the *ex-officio* chairman of the parochial church council, which may also include other *ex-officio* members, and co-opted members, in addition to the elected members. The council is a body corporate with perpetual succession. It therefore has a legal existence apart from the members who compose

[1] See pp. 10, 14 and 17 *ante.*

it. To it have been transferred (amongst other powers) all the powers which, until the coming into force of the Parochial Church Council (Powers) Measure 1921, were vested in the churchwardens in relation to (a) the financial affairs of the church, (b) the care, maintenance and insurance of the fabric of the church and its goods and ornaments, and (c) the care and maintenance of the churchyard (open or closed), with all the rights previously possessed by the churchwardens to recover from the local authority the cost of maintaining a closed church-yard.[1]

The powers conferred on the council, as distinct from those transferred to it, include the power to acquire, manage and administer property for ecclesiastical purposes affecting the parish, power to frame an annual budget of moneys required for maintenance of church work, power to levy and collect a voluntary church rate, and power to make representations to the bishop with regard to any matter affecting the welfare of the church in the parish.

The council is also given power, jointly with the incumbent, to appoint and dismiss the parish clerk and sexton and to determine the salaries and conditions of service of these officers, and to determine the objects to which money collected in church (other than alms taken at the Communion Service) are to be allocated.

All the powers so far mentioned are contained in the Parochial Church Council (Powers) Measure 1956. There follow some examples of powers and functions conferred on parochial church councils by various other legislative provisions:

(i) Under section 45 of the Ecclesiastical Dilapidations Measure 1923, a council may pay or promise to pay any money in discharge or reduction of a liability incurred by virtue of an order made under the Measure (in respect of work required to be done to the parsonage house or other benefice buildings).

(ii) A council is entitled to object to a proposal under the Parsonage Measure 1938 for the sale or pulling down of a residence house belonging to the benefice, or for the erection or purchase of a new residence house. Any such objection

---

[1] See further as to this, p. 115 *post*.

must be considered by the Church Commissioners before consenting to the proposal.

(iii) A parochial church council is given certain rights on the occurrence of a vacancy in the benefice by the Benefices (Exercise of Rights of Presentation) Measure 1931; and in respect of a proposed transfer of the right of patronage by the Benefices (Transfer of Rights of Patronage) Measure 1930. These rights are considered in detail in Chapter VII *ante.*

(iv) The council's consent is necessary to the use of a form or draft of a form of service approved under the Prayer Book (Alternative and Other Services) Measure 1965; also to the use in church of versions of the Bible whose use has been authorised under the Prayer Book (Versions of the Bible) Measure 1965. And under the Vestures of Ministers Measure 1964, an incumbent is not permitted to change the form of vesture already in use without first consulting the council, and, in the case of disagreement on the part of the council, referring the matter to the bishop.

(v) Under the Pastoral Measure 1968, the parochial church council of any parish which is liable to be affected by a proposed pastoral scheme or order is an 'interested party' whose views must be ascertained, and to whom an opportunity must be given of meeting the Pastoral Committee or a subcommittee or representative thereof. On the preparation of the draft scheme or order by the Church Commissioners, a copy of the draft must be sent to the council, together with a notice stating that written representations with respect to it must be made within a specified time, not being less than twenty-eight days.

(vi) Under the Sharing of Church Buildings Act 1969, when the Church of England is concerned in a 'sharing agreement' relating to any church building, the parochial church council of the parish in which the building is situated is a necessary party to the agreement.

(vii) Under the new code of Canons (Canons F1 to F14) the parochial church council is charged with the provision of certain requisites of divine service. The articles so prescribed include a font, a holy table, communion plate, communion linen, surplices for the minister, a reading desk and a pulpit, seats for the congregation, church bells, a large Bible and Prayer Book and a pulpit Bible, an alms box, register books, and a service book and banns book. The council is also charged by the same canons with the general duty of the care and repair of all churches, chapels and churchyards within the parish.

With respect to team and group ministries established by pastoral schemes, and with respect also to new parishes created by pastoral schemes, and to cases where there are two or more parishes within the area of a single benefice or where two or more benefices are held in plurality, the Pastoral Measure 1968 contains special provisions relating to the parochial church meetings and councils of the parishes concerned. The text of these provisions is set out later in this Chapter.

## (2) THE CHURCH REPRESENTATION RULES (SO FAR AS RELATING TO PAROCHIAL CHURCH MEETINGS AND COUNCILS) WITH NOTES[1]

### PART I

### CHURCH ELECTORAL ROLL

#### *Formation of Roll*

**1.** (1) There shall be a church electoral roll (in these rules referred to as "the roll") in every parish, on which the names of lay persons shall be entered as hereinafter provided. The roll shall be available for inspection by bona-fide inquirers.

(2) A lay person shall be entitled to have his name entered on the electoral roll of a parish, if he—

(*a*) is baptised;

(*b*) is a member of the Church of England or another Church of the Anglican Communion or an overseas Church in

1 The Church Representation Rules constitute Schedule 3 to the Synodical Government Measure 1969. They relate not only to representation at the parish level but also to deanery and diocesan synods and the General Synod. For reasons of space, the text is here reproduced only of those Rules which are relevant to representation at the parish level. The general effect of those Rules which relate exclusively to the synods is summarised in Chapter II *ante*.

communion with the Church of England, and is not a member of any other religious body which is not in communion with the Church of England;[1]

(c) is of seventeen years or upwards;

(d) is resident in the parish, or, if not so resident, has habitually attended public worship in the parish during a period of six months prior to enrolment; and

(e) has signed the form of application for enrolment set out in section 1 of Appendix I to these rules.

(3) No person shall be entitled to have his name on the roll of more than one parish at the same time:

Provided that where:—

(a) a person has the qualifications required under these rules for having his name on the roll of two parishes;[2]

(b) his name is on the roll of one of those parishes;

(c) he applies in accordance with these rules to have his name entered on the roll of the other parish;

(d) the parochial church councils of both parishes consent to his name being on the roll of both parishes;

then, for so long as he retains the necessary qualifications, he shall be entitled to have his name on the roll of both the parishes concerned. The granting of such consent shall be in the discretion of the councils hereinbefore mentioned, and there shall be no right of appeal if it is withheld.

No person shall in any circumstances be entitled to have his name on the roll of more than two parishes at the same time.

(4) The roll shall, until a parochial church council has been constituted in a parish, be formed and revised by the minister and churchwardens (if any), and shall, after such council has been constituted, be kept and revised by or under the direction of the council. Reference in this rule to a parochial church council shall, so far as may be necessary for giving effect to these rules, be construed as including references to the minister and churchwardens (if any).

[1] Previously to these Rules, membership of the Church of England was an essential qualification.

[2] It is legally possible for a person to be 'resident' in two places at once, e.g. if he has a house in each place and regularly lives in each house for a substantial part of the year. Thus the qualification of being 'resident' may be satisfied simultaneously as regards each of the two parishes in question. But see Rule 44(5) (p. 103 *post*).

(5) The parochial church council shall appoint an electoral roll officer to act under its directions for the purpose of carrying out its functions with regard to the electoral roll.[1]

(6) The names of persons who are entitled to have their names entered upon the roll of the parish shall, subject to the provisions of these rules, be from time to time added to the roll. No name shall be added to or removed from the roll except by the authority of the parochial church council and it shall be the duty of that council to keep the roll constantly up to date and to cause names to be added and removed as from time to time required by these rules.

(7) Subject to the provisions of this rule, a person's name shall, as the occasion arises, be removed from the roll, if he:—

(a) has died; or

(b) becomes a clerk in Holy Orders; or

(c) signifies in writing his desire that his name should be removed; or

(d) becomes a member of any religious body which is not in communion with the Church of England; or

(e) ceases to reside in the parish, unless after so ceasing he continues habitually to attend public worship in the parish; or

(f) is not resident in the parish and has not attended public worship in the parish during the preceding six months, not having been prevented from doing so by illness or other sufficient cause; or

(g) at any time after the entry of his name on the roll has his name entered on the roll of another parish except in accordance with the proviso to paragraph (3) of this rule; or

(h) was not entitled to have his name entered on the roll at the time when it was entered.

(8) The removal of a person's name from the roll under any of the provisions of these rules shall be without prejudice to his right to have his name entered again, if he is entitled to do so.

(9) The roll shall where practicable contain a record of the address of every person whose name is entered on the roll, but a failure to comply with this requirement shall not prejudice the validity of any entry on the roll.

---

[1] Previously to these Rules the appointment of an electoral roll officer was not an absolute legal requirement, though in practice many councils did appoint such an officer.

## *Revision of Roll and Preparation of New Roll*

**2.** (1) Except in a year in which a new roll is prepared, the roll of a parish shall be revised annually by or under the direction of the council. Notice of the intended revision in the form set out in section 2 of Appendix I to these rules shall be affixed by the minister or under his direction on or near the principal door of every church in the parish and every building in the parish licensed for public worship and remain so affixed for a period of not less than fourteen days before the commencement of the revision. The revision shall be completed not less than fifteen days or more than twenty-eight days before the annual parochial church meeting.

(2) Upon every revision all enrolments or removals from the roll which have been effected since the date of the last revision (or since the formation of the roll, if there has been no previous revision) shall be reviewed, and such further enrolments or removals from the rolls as may be required shall be effected.

(3) After the completion of the revision, a copy of the roll as revised shall, together with a list of the names removed from the roll since the last revision (or since the formation of the roll, if there has been no previous revision), be published by being exhibited continuously for not less than fourteen days before the annual parochial church meeting on or near the principal door of the parish church in such manner as the council shall appoint. No name shall be entered upon or removed from the roll during the period in any year between the completion of the revision and the close of the annual parochial church meeting.

(4)[1] Not less than two months before the annual parochial church meeting in the year 1972 and every succeeding sixth year notice in the form set out in section 3 of Appendix 1 to these rules shall be affixed by the minister or under his direction on or

[1] Sub-paragraphs (4) to (7) provide for the preparation of an entirely new electoral roll in every parish in the year 1972, and in every succeeding sixth year. On every such occasion, every person whose name was entered on the previous roll must make a fresh application in order to be entered on the new roll. The requirement of a new roll at intervals of six years was imposed for the first time by these Rules. Its object is to procure a periodical re-checking of every single name on the roll, and thus to ensure (as far as possible) the exclusion of all disqualified persons and of all persons who have ceased to take an active interest in Church affairs.

near the principal door of every church in the parish and every building in the parish licensed for public worship and remain so affixed for a period of not less than fourteen days. On the affixing of the notice a new roll shall be prepared.

(5) The parochial church council shall be responsible for ensuring that all persons whose names are entered on the previous electoral roll are informed of the preparation of the new roll either by the notice affixed under the preceding paragraph, or by public announcement, or by communication in writing or verbally to the person concerned.

(6) The new roll shall be prepared by entering upon it the names of persons entitled to entry under rule 1(2), and a fresh application shall be required from persons whose names were entered on the previous roll. A person whose name was so entered shall not be disqualified for entry on the new roll by reason only of his failure to comply with the conditions specified in rule 1(2)(*d*), if he was prevented from doing so by illness or other sufficient cause, and the circumstances shall be stated on the application form. The preparation of the new roll shall be completed not less than fifteen days or more than twenty-eight days before the annual parochial church meeting.

(7) After the completion of the new roll, a copy shall be published by being exhibited continuously for not less than fourteen days before the annual parochial church meeting on or near the principal door of the parish church in such manner as the council shall appoint. No name shall be entered upon or removed from the roll during the period in any year between the completion of the new roll and the close of the annual parochial church meeting. On the publication of the new roll the previous roll shall cease to have effect.

(8) Upon the alteration of the boundaries of any parishes the parochial church council of the parish from which any area is transferred shall enquire from the persons resident in that area whose names are entered on the roll of the parish, whether they wish to have their names transferred to the roll of the other parish. The parochial church council shall remove the names of persons answering in the affirmative from its own roll and shall inform the parochial church council of the parish in which such persons now reside, which shall enter the names on its roll without any application for enrolment being required.

*Procedural provisions relating to entry and removal of names*

**3.** (1) When a person applying for enrolment on the roll of any parish signifies his desire that his name should be removed from the roll of any other parish, notice of that fact shall be sent by the parochial church council receiving the application to the parochial church council of that other parish.

(2) When the name of any person is removed from the roll of the parish owing to his having become resident in another parish, notice of that fact shall, whenever possible, be sent by the parochial church council of the first mentioned parish to the parochial church council of the last mentioned parish.

(3) When a person wishes to have his name on the rolls of two parishes in accordance with rule 1(3), his name must first be on the roll of one of those two parishes.

He must then:—

(a) apply to the parochial church council of that parish for its consent to his name being entered on the roll of the other parish concerned; and

(b) if such consent is given, apply for entry on the roll of the other parish concerned.

The parochial church council of that other parish shall then decide whether or not to give its consent to his name being on the roll of both parishes and, if it does not give consent, the application for entry on the roll of that parish shall be refused.[1]

(4) For so long as the name of any person is on the roll of two parishes pursuant to rule 1(3), a note to that effect shall be entered upon the roll of each of the parishes concerned. Where consent is given by the parochial church council of the parish to an

[1] On the occasion of the preparation of a new roll under paragraphs (4) to (7) of Rule 2, a person who wishes to have his name on the rolls of two parishes must in the first place apply to have it entered on the roll of one of them. When the parochial church council of that parish has been elected on the basis of the new roll, he may then apply to it for consent to his name being entered on the roll of the other parish. If such consent is given he then applies to the council of the other parish for entry of his name on the roll of that other parish, and it is for the council of that other parish to decide whether it will also consent.

The fact that the person in question previously had his name duly entered on the rolls of both parishes does not entitle him as of right to be entered on the new rolls of both of them. The necessary consents must be obtained afresh.

application under sub-paragraph (*a*) of the preceding paragraph such note may be added immediately on the roll of that parish, but if so added, must be cancelled immediately on notification being given that the parochial church council of the other parish concerned has refused its consent to the name of the person in question being on the rolls of both parishes.

(5) An omission to comply with the requirements of this rule shall not disqualify any person whose name has been entered upon any roll.

## *Certification of Numbers on Rolls*[1]

**4.** (1) Not later than the first day of July—

(*a*) in any year immediately preceding a year in which elections of members of deanery synods or diocesan synods will fall due,

(*b*) in any year being the fourth year after the last preceding election of members of the House of Laity of the General Synod,

the number of names on the roll of each parish shall be certified to the secretary of the diocesan synod and the secretary of the deanery synod, and the certificate shall be signed by the chairman, vice-chairman, secretary or electoral roll officer of the parochial church council:

Provided that, if the General Synod is at any time dissolved before the fourth year after the last preceding election of the House of Laity or before this rule has taken effect during that year, the General Synod or the Presidents thereof may give directions requiring the number of names on the roll of each parish to be certified as aforesaid within such time as may be specified, and the directions may, if the dissolution is known to be impending, be given before it occurs.

[1] Rule 4 is necessary because the number of lay representatives elected by a parish to a deanery synod depends on the number of persons on the electoral roll of the parish: and similarly, the number of lay representatives elected by a deanery to a diocesan synod, or by a diocese to the General Synod, depends on the aggregate number of the names on the rolls of all the parishes in the deanery or the diocese (as the case may be). It is therefore necessary that the officials concerned with the elections to these respective synods should be furnished with the number of the names on the roll of each relevant parish, as on a date as near as practicable to the time of an election.

(2) A copy of such certificate shall be affixed at or near to the principal door of every church in the parish and every building licensed for public worship in the parish when the certificate is sent to the secretary of the diocesan synod, and shall remain so affixed for a period of not less than fourteen days.

(3) Every certificate under this rule shall include a special statement certifying how many of the total number of names included in the certificate relate to persons whose names are entered on the rolls of two parishes.[1]

(4) In calculating for the purposes of these rules the number of names on the roll of the parish or on the rolls of the parishes in the deanery or diocese the person who receives the certificate shall adjust the total number of names certified by deducting therefrom one half of the number of names included in the special statement.

(5) Any question as to the accuracy of any certificate given under this rule shall be decided in such manner as the diocesan synod or the bishop's council and standing committee shall determine.

## PART II

## PAROCHIAL CHURCH MEETINGS AND COUNCILS ANNUAL MEETINGS

**5.** (1) In every parish there shall be held not later than the 30th April in each year[2] the annual parochial church meeting (hereafter in these rules referred to as "the annual meeting").

(2) All lay persons whose names are entered on the roll of the parish shall be entitled to attend the annual meeting and to take part in its proceedings, and no other lay person shall be so entitled.[3]

---

[1] For the purpose of calculating the number of lay representatives to be elected to any synod, any person whose name is entered on the rolls of two parishes counts as half a person only in each parish.

[2] Previously to these Rules, the meeting had to be held 'not later in the year than the week following Easter week'.

[3] If, as is frequently the arrangement, the meeting immediately follows the meeting of the parishioners for the appointment of churchwardens, lay persons entitled to attend the meeting of parishioners, but who are not on the electoral roll, should be called upon to leave at the end of the meeting of parishioners.

(3) A clerk in Holy Orders shall be entitled to attend the annual meeting of a parish and take part in its proceedings—

(*a*) if he is either beneficed in or licensed to the parish or any other parish in the area of the benefice to which the parish belongs; or

(*b*) if the parish is in the area of a group ministry and he is an incumbent of any benefice in the group; or

(*c*) if he is resident in the parish and is not beneficed in or licensed to any other parish.[1]

### Convening of Meeting

**6.** (1) The annual meeting shall be convened by the minister of the parish by a notice in the form set out in section 4 of Appendix 1 to these rules affixed on or near to the principal door of every church in the parish and every building licensed for public worship in the parish, for a period including the last two Sundays before the day of the meeting.

(2) The annual meeting shall be held at such place on such date and at such hour as shall be directed by the previous annual meeting, or by the parochial church council (which may vary any direction given by a previous annual meeting) or in the absence of any such direction as shall be appointed by the minister.

(3) During the vacancy of the benefice or curacy or when the minister is absent or incapacitated by illness or any other cause, the vice-chairman of the parochial church council, or if there is no vice-chairman, or if he is unable or unwilling to act, the secretary of or some other person appointed by that council shall have all the powers vested in the minister under this rule.

(4) The annual meeting shall be held at a place within the parish unless the parochial church council decide otherwise.

### Chairman

**7.** The minister, if present, or if he is not present, the vice-

[1] Section 45 of the Cathedrals Measure 1963 provides that residentiary and minor canons of a parish church cathedral may attend the annual parochial church meeting of the parish of that cathedral, whether or not they are resident in the parish. This section is not expressly repealed, and it would seem that the clergy in question still have this right, even though, if not resident in the parish, they do not come within any of the categories specified in this rule.

chairman of the parochial church council, or, if he also is not present, a chairman chosen by the annual meeting shall preside thereat. In case of an equal division of votes, the chairman of the meeting shall have a second or casting vote; but no clerical chairman shall have a vote in the election of the parochial representatives of the laity. [1]

## Business

**8.** (1) The annual meeting shall receive from the parochial church council and shall be free to discuss:—

(*a*) a copy or copies of the roll;

(*b*) an annual report on the proceedings of the parochial church council;

(*c*) an annual report on the financial affairs of the parish;

(*d*) the audited accounts of the parochial church council for the year ending on the 31st December immediately preceding the meeting;

(*e*) an audited statement of the funds and property, if any, remaining in the hands of the parochial church council at the said date;

(*f*) a report upon the fabric, goods and ornaments of the church or churches of the parish; and

(*g*) a report on the proceedings of the deanery synod.

(2) The council shall cause a copy of the said audited accounts and the said audited statement to be affixed on or near the principal door of every church in the parish and every building licensed for public worship in the parish at least seven days before the annual meeting.

(3) Such accounts and statement shall be submitted to the annual meeting for approval. If approved, they shall be signed by the chairman of the meeting, who shall then deliver them to the parochial church council for publication, and the parochial church council shall forthwith cause them to be published and

---

[1] Previously to these Rules, a clerical chairman was permitted a casting vote in an election though not an original vote, but now the casting vote is also disallowed and where there is an equality of votes the decision is by lot; see Rule 10(8) *post*. That the spin of a coin should be preferred to the wisdom of the presiding cleric may be thought a somewhat extreme application of the principle of excluding all clerical influence in the election of lay representatives.

G

affixed on or near the principal door of every church in the parish and every building licensed for public worship in the parish and at such other conspicuous place or places in the parish as the parochial church council think appropriate.

(4) The annual meeting shall in the manner provided by rule 10 of these rules:—

(*a*) elect in every third year parochial representatives of the laity to the deanery synod;

(*b*) elect parochial representatives of the laity to the parochial church council;

(*c*) elect sidesmen;[1]

and the elections shall be carried out in the above order.

(5) The annual meeting shall appoint the auditors to the council.

(6) Any person entitled to attend the annual meeting may ask any question about parochial church matters, or bring about a discussion of any matter of parochial or general church interest, by moving a general resolution or by moving to give any particular recommendation to the council in relation to its duties.

(7) The annual meeting shall have power to adjourn and to determine its own rules of procedure.

(8) The secretary of the parochial church council (or another person appointed by the meeting in his place) shall act as a clerk of the annual meeting, and shall record the minutes thereof.

## *Qualifications of persons to be chosen or elected by annual meetings*

**9.** (1) The qualifications of a person to be elected a parochial representative of the laity to either of the bodies referred to in the last preceding rule[2] are that—

(*a*) his name is entered on the roll of the parish; and

(*b*) he is an actual communicant member of the Church of England or, in the case of election to the parochial church council, of any other Church of the Anglican Communion

[1] The election of sidesmen is in fact optional. Under the Rules previously in force, the sidesmen (if any) were elected by the annual meeting and the minister; and if the meeting and the minister could not agree, half were elected by the meeting and the other half appointed by the minister. Now all are elected by the meeting and the minister is excluded from any vote.

[2] i.e. the deanery synod and the parochial church council.

or of an overseas Church in communion with the Church of England; and

(c) in the case of election to the deanery synod, he is of age to vote at a Parliamentary election:[1]

Provided that—

(i) if his name is entered on the rolls of two parishes, he must choose one of those parishes for the purpose of qualification for election to a deanery synod, but may serve on the parochial church councils of both parishes;

(ii) the registrar of the diocese shall not be qualified for election to any of the said bodies in that diocese.

(2) The qualification of a person to be elected a sidesman is that his name is entered on the roll of the parish.

(3) No person shall be elected under the last preceding rule unless he has signified his consent to serve or there is in the opinion of the meeting sufficient evidence of his willingness to serve.

## Conduct of Elections at Annual Meetings

**10.** (1) This rule shall apply to all elections at annual meetings.

(2) All candidates for election at an annual meeting must be nominated and seconded by persons entitled to attend the annual meeting, and in the case of parochial representatives of the laity, by persons whose names are entered on the roll of the parish. A candidate shall be nominated or seconded either before the meeting in writing or at the meeting.

(3) If the number of candidates nominated is not greater than the number of seats to be filled, the candidates nominated shall forthwith be declared elected.

(4) If more candidates are nominated than there are seats to be filled, the election shall take place at the annual meeting.

(5) No clerk in Holy Orders shall be entitled to vote in the election of any parochial representative of the laity.[2]

(6) Each person entitled to vote shall have as many votes as

[1] Previously to these Rules, the age qualification was the same for membership of the parochial church council; but now a person, otherwise qualified, may become a member of the council after attaining the age of seventeen.

[2] Previously to these Rules, a clerical chairman had a casting though not an original vote.

there are seats to be filled but may not give more than one vote to any one candidate.

(7) Votes may be given:—

(*a*) on voting papers, which must be signed by the voter; or

(*b*) if no person present objects thereto, by show of hands.

(8) Where owing to an equality of votes an election is not decided, the decision between the persons for whom the equal numbers of votes have been cast shall be taken by lot.

(9) The result of any election by an annual meeting shall be announced as soon as practicable by the person presiding over the election, and a notice of the result shall in every case be affixed on or near the principal door of every church in the parish and every building licensed for public worship in the parish, and shall bear the date on which the result is declared. The notice shall remain affixed for not less than fourteen days.

(10) Returns of parochial representatives of the laity elected to the deanery synod shall be sent to the secretary of that synod.

## CONDUCT OF ELECTIONS OF CHURCHWARDENS

**11.** (1) If elections of churchwardens take place at meetings of parishioners under section 3 of the Churchwardens (Appointment and Resignation) Measure 1964[1] either because there has been no joint consent under section 2 of that Measure or because there is no minister, the elections shall be conducted, announced and notified in the same manner as elections under the preceding rule except that all persons entitled to attend the meeting of parishioners other than the minister shall be entitled to nominate and vote at such elections of churchwardens.

(2) The Churchwardens (Appointment and Resignation) Measure 1964 shall be amended as follows:—

(*a*) in section 2(1) for the words "not later in the year than during the week following Easter week" there shall be substituted the words "not later than the 30th April in each year";

(*b*) sections 4, 5, 6 and 11(3) shall be repealed; and

(*c*) section 3(6) shall not apply to elections of churchwardens.

[1] See p. 55 *ante* for the text of this Measure and notes thereto. The amendments effected by these Rules are there indicated by appropriate alterations of the text and by explanatory notes.

## PAROCHIAL CHURCH COUNCIL

### *Members*

**12.** (1) The parochial church council shall consist of:—

(*a*) all clerks in Holy Orders beneficed in or licensed to the parish, including in the case of a team ministry all vicars in the team;

(*b*) any deaconess or woman worker licensed to the parish or any male lay worker licensed to the parish and receiving a stipend in respect of work for the cure of souls in the parish;

(*c*) the churchwardens, being actual communicant members of the Church of England whose names are on the roll of the parish;

(*d*) any reader whose name is on the roll of the parish, if the annual meeting so determines;

(*e*) all persons whose names are on the roll of the parish and who are lay members of any deanery synod, diocesan synod or the General Synod;

(*f*) such number of representatives of the laity as the annual meeting may decide, and so that the number determined may be altered from time to time by a resolution passed at any annual meeting, but such resolution shall not take effect before the next ensuing annual meeting; and

(*g*) co-opted members, if the parochial church council so decides, not exceeding in number one-fifth of the representatives of the laity elected under the last preceding sub-paragraph of this paragraph, and being either clerks in Holy Orders or actual lay communicant members of the Church of England of seventeen years of age or upwards. The term of office of a co-opted member shall be until the conclusion of the next annual meeting; but without prejudice to his being co-opted on subsequent occasions for a similar term, subject to and in accordance with the provisions of these rules.

(2) Any elected representative of the laity whose name is removed from the roll under rule 1 shall forthwith cease to be a member of the parochial church council, without prejudice to any right that the council may have to make him a co-opted member: provided that, where a person's name is removed from the roll under sub-paragraph (*c*) of rule 1(7) he shall not cease

to be a member of the council by virtue of that fact unless the council so resolves.

(3) Where a group ministry is established the incumbents of all benefices in the group shall be entitled to attend meetings of the parochial church councils of all the parishes in the area for which the group ministry is established. They shall be entitled to receive documents circulated to members of councils of which they are not themselves members and to speak but not to vote at meetings of such councils.

## *General Provisions relating to Parochial Church Councils*

**13.** The provisions in Appendix II to these rules shall have effect with respect to parochial church councils, and with respect to the officers, the meetings and the proceedings thereof:

Provided that a parochial church council may, with the consent of the diocesan synod, vary the said provisions, in their application to the council.

## *Term of office*

**14.** Representatives of the laity on the parochial church council of a parish shall hold office from the conclusion of the annual meeting until the conclusion of the next annual meeting of the parish:

Provided that the annual meeting may decide that one-third only (or the number nearest to one-third) of the representatives of the laity elected to the council shall retire from office in every year. In any case where it is so decided, the representatives of the laity to retire from office at each annual meeting shall be those who have been longest in office since last elected,[1] and as between representatives of the laity elected on the same day, those to retire shall (unless they otherwise agree among themselves) be selected by lot. A representative of the laity shall in any event retire at the conclusion of the third annual meeting after that at which he was elected.

---

[1] This provision takes effect subject to Rule 39(4) under which, when a person has been elected to fill a casual vacancy, he holds office only for the unexpired portion of the term of office of the person in whose place he was elected (see p. 100 *post*).

## *Limitation on years of service*

**15.** The annual meeting may decide that no representative of the laity on the parochial church council may hold office for more than a specified number of years continuously and may also decide that after a specified interval a person who has ceased to be eligible by reason of such decision may again stand for election as a representative of the laity on the council.[1]

## *Parishes with more than one Place of Worship*

**16.** (1) In any parish where there are two or more churches or buildings licensed for public worship the annual meeting may make a scheme, either:—

(*a*) for the election of representatives of the laity to the parochial church council in such manner as to ensure due representation of the congregation of each such church or building; or

(*b*) for the election of district church councils for any district in the parish in which a church (other than the parish church) or building licensed as aforesaid is situated.[2]

(2) A scheme for the election of any district church council or councils under the preceding paragraph shall provide for the election of representatives of the laity on to such council, for ex-officio members and for the chairmanship of such council and shall contain such other provisions as to membership and procedure as shall be considered appropriate by the annual meeting.

(3) Such a scheme may also provide for the delegation by the parochial church council to a district church council of such functions as it may specify and subject to the scheme the parochial church council may delegate to a district church council such of its functions as it shall think fit.

(4) Such a scheme may also provide for the election or choice of one or two deputy churchwardens in respect of any such church or building, and for the delegation to him or them of such functions of the churchwardens relating to that church or

[1] This power is newly conferred by these Rules.

[2] The power to establish 'district church councils' with or without 'deputy churchwardens', otherwise than in the case of team ministries, is newly conferred by these Rules.

building as the scheme may specify, and the churchwardens may, subject to the scheme, delegate such of their said functions as they think fit to the deputy churchwarden or churchwardens.

(5) No scheme under this rule shall be valid unless approved by at least two-thirds of the persons present and voting at the annual meeting, nor shall it be operative until the next ensuing annual meeting. Every such scheme shall, on its approval, be communicated to the secretary of the diocesan synod, who may if he considers it appropriate lay the scheme before the bishop's council and standing committee of that synod, which may determine that the scheme shall not come into operation.

(6) This rule shall be without prejudice to the establishment of a district church council and deputy churchwardens in the area of a team ministry by a scheme or by an instrument made by the bishop under paragraph 3(2) of Schedule 3 to the Pastoral Measure 1968,[1] or to the appointment, in parishes with more than one parish church, of two churchwardens for each parish church under section 27(3) of the said Measure.[2]

## *Joint Parochial Church Councils and Group Councils*

**17.** These rules shall, in relation to a joint parochial church council established by a scheme or order under paragraph 13 of Schedule 3 to the Pastoral Measure 1968, have effect subject to the scheme or order, and, in relation to a group council established by a scheme or an instrument of the bishop under paragraph 3(4) of the said Schedule, have effect subject to the scheme or instrument.[3]

## SPECIAL AND EXTRAORDINARY MEETINGS

**18.** (1) In addition to the annual meeting, the minister of a parish may convene a special parochial church meeting, and he shall do so on a written representation by not less than one-third of the lay members of the parochial church council; and the provisions of these rules relating to the convening and conduct of

[1] See p. 123 *post* for the text of this provision.

[2] As to such appointments, see p. 56 *ante*.

[3] For the text of the provisions of the Pastoral Measure 1968 referred to in this Rule, see pp. 124 and 125 *post*.

the annual meeting shall, with the necessary modifications, apply to a special parochial church meeting.

(2) On a written representation made to the archdeacon by not less than one-third of the lay members of the parochial church council, or by one-tenth of the persons whose names are on the roll of the parish, and deemed by the archdeacon to have been made with sufficient cause, the archdeacon shall convene an extraordinary meeting of the parochial church council or an extraordinary parochial church meeting, and shall either take the chair himself or shall appoint a chairman to preside. The chairman, not being otherwise entitled to attend such meeting, shall not be entitled to vote upon any resolution before the meeting.

(3) In any case where the archdeacon is himself the minister, any representation under paragraph (2) of this rule shall be made to the bishop, and in any such case the references to the archdeacon in paragraph (2) of this rule shall be construed as references to the bishop, or to a person appointed by him to act on his behalf.

(4) The persons entitled to attend any special or extraordinary parochial church meeting shall be those entitled to attend the annual meeting.

PARTS III, IV AND V . . .[1]

## PART VI

## APPEALS AND DISQUALIFICATIONS

### *Appeals*

**36.** (1) Subject to the provisions of rule 1(3) of these rules there shall be a right of appeal by any person aggrieved against:—

(*a*) any enrolment, or refusal of enrolment, on the roll of a parish;

(*b*) the removal of any name, or the refusal to remove any name, from the roll of a parish;

[1] Parts III, IV, and V of the Rules (comprising Rules 19 to 35) relate exclusively to deanery synods, diocesan synods and the General Synod, and are here omitted.

(c) the allowance or disallowance of any vote given or tendered in an election under these rules or to a body constituted under or in accordance with these rules;

(d) the result of any election or choice held or made or purporting to be held or made under these rules, or any election or choice of members of a body constituted under or in accordance with these rules.

(2) In the case of an appeal arising out of an election to the House of Laity of the General Synod or the diocesan synod notice of the appeal shall be given in writing to the bishop. In any other case, notice of the appeal shall be given in writing to the rural dean, or, if there be no rural dean, to the archdeacon. Notices under this paragraph shall be given:—

(a) in the case of an appeal against an enrolment or a refusal of an enrolment, or in the case of an appeal against the removal of any name or the refusal to remove any name from the roll, not later than fourteen days after the date of the enrolment, removal or refusal or, if the appeal arises on the revision of the roll or the preparation of a new roll, not later than fourteen days after the first publication of the revised or new roll under rule 2(3) or (7);

(b) in the case of an appeal against the allowance or disallowance of a vote, not later than fourteen days after such allowance or disallowance;

(c) in the case of an appeal against the result of an election, not later than fourteen days after the result thereof has been announced by the presiding officer.

(3) An error in the electoral roll shall not be a ground of appeal against the result of any election unless—

(i) either it has been determined under this rule that there has been such an error or the question is awaiting determination under this rule; and

(ii) the error would or might be material to the result of the election;

and the allowance or disallowance of a vote shall not be a ground of appeal against the result of an election unless the allowance or disallowance would or might be material to the result of the election.

(4) An appeal arising out of an election or choice of members of the House of Laity of the General Synod shall be referred to

the standing committee of the Synod who shall appoint two or more of their members to consider and decide the appeal.

(5) In each diocese there shall be an electoral commission constituted by the diocesan synod. The bishop or the archdeacon or the rural dean, as the case may be, shall, unless the parties agree to a settlement of their dispute, refer any appeal under this rule except an appeal arising out of an election to the House of Laity to the commission. The commission shall appoint two or more of its members to consider and decide any appeal so referred. All or the majority of the members appointed shall be laymen, save when the question arises in connection with an election or choice of members of the house of clergy of the diocesan synod or a deanery synod when all or the majority so appointed shall be clerks in Holy Orders. The decision of such members shall be final.

(6) For the purpose of the consideration and decision of any appeal under this rule, the members of the standing committee or commission so appointed shall consider all the relevant circumstances, and shall be entitled to inspect all documents and papers relating to the subject matter of the appeal, and be furnished with all information respecting the same which they may require. They shall give to the parties to the appeal an opportunity of appearing before them in person or through a legal or other representative.

(7) The members of the standing committee or the commission appointed in any diocese under this rule shall have power at any time to extend the time within which a notice of appeal is given.

**37.** . . .[1]

### *Ex-Officio Membership not to Disqualify for Election*

**38.** No lay person shall be disqualified from being elected or chosen a member of any body under these rules by the fact that he is also a member ex-officio of that body; and no lay person shall be deemed to vacate his seat as such an elected or chosen member of any body by reason only of the fact that subsequently to his election or choice he has become a member of that body ex-officio.

---

[1] Rule 37 relates exclusively to vacation of membership of a deanery or diocesan synod or of the General Synod, and is here omitted.

## PART VII

## SUPPLEMENTARY AND INTERPRETATION

### *Casual Vacancies*

**39.** (1) Elections to fill casual vacancies among persons elected under these rules shall be conducted in the same manner as ordinary elections, a special meeting of the electing body being held, if necessary, for the purpose, provided that in the case of a casual vacancy among the parochial representatives elected to the parochial church council or deanery synod, such vacancy may be filled by the parochial church council. Such elections shall, where possible, be held at such times as will enable all casual vacancies among representatives of the laity who are electors to be filled at the time of every election to the House of Laity of the General Synod, but so that no such election shall be invalid by reason of any casual vacancies not having been so filled up.

(2) Elections to fill casual vacancies shall be held as soon as reasonably practicable after the vacancy has occurred, and elections to fill a casual vacancy in the House of Laity of the General Synod or either house of the diocesan synod shall be completed within six months from the occurrence of the vacancy: Provided that where a casual vacancy occurs in any of these three houses and the period for holding a general election to that house is due to begin within nine months of the vacancy, such vacancy shall not be filled unless the bishop so directs.

(3) The preceding provisions of this rule shall apply, so far as applicable and with the necessary modifications, to the choosing of persons under these rules as it applies to the election of persons thereunder, and shall also apply to the election or choosing of members of any body constituted under or in accordance with these rules.

(4) Any person elected or chosen to fill a casual vacancy shall hold office only for the unexpired portion of the term of office of the person in whose place he is elected or chosen.

### *Resignations*

**40.** Persons holding office under these rules or members of bodies constituted by or in accordance with these rules may resign at will.[1]

## *Notices*

**41.** Any notice or other document required or authorised to be sent or given under these rules shall be deemed to have been duly sent or given if sent through the post addressed to the person to whom it is required or authorised to be sent or given at that person's last known address.

## *Revocation and Variation of Rules, etc.*

**42.** Subject to the provisions of these rules any power conferred by these rules to make, approve, frame, pass or adopt any rule, order, resolution, determination, decision, appointment or scheme, or to give any consent or settle any constitution, or to prescribe the manner of doing anything, shall be construed as including a power, exercisable in a like manner and subject to the like conditions, to revoke or vary any such rule, order, resolution, determination, decision, appointment, scheme, consent or constitution, or anything so prescribed.

## *Special Provisions*

**43.** (1) In the carrying out of these rules in any diocese the bishop of such diocese shall have power:—
(*a*) to make provision for any matter not herein provided for;
(*b*) to appoint a person to do any act in respect of which there has been any neglect or default on the part of any person or body charged with any duty under these rules;
(*c*) so far as may be necessary for the purpose of giving effect to the intention of these rules, to extend or alter the time for holding any meeting or election or to modify the procedure laid down by these rules in connection therewith;
(*d*) in any case in which there has been no valid election, to direct a fresh election to be held and to give such directions in connection therewith as he may think necessary; and
(*e*) in any case in which any difficulties arise, to give any direc-

[1] Previously to these Rules, the resignation of a member of the parochial church council required the consent of the council, but this is no longer so.

tions which he may consider expedient for the purpose of removing the difficulties.

(2) The powers of the bishop under this rule shall not enable him:—

(*a*) to validate anything that was invalid at the time when it was done;

(*b*) to give any direction that is contrary to any resolution of the General Synod.

(3) No proceedings of any body constituted under these rules shall be invalidated by any vacancy in the membership of that body or by any defect in the qualification, election or appointment of any members thereof.

(4) No proceedings shall be invalidated by the use of a form which differs from that prescribed by these rules if the form which has in fact been used is to a substantially similar effect. Any question as to whether the form which has been used is to a substantially similar effect shall be determined by the bishop.

(5) In the case of an omission in any parish to prepare or maintain a roll or form or maintain a council or to hold the annual meeting, the rural dean upon such omission being brought to his notice shall ascertain and report to the bishop the cause thereof.

(6) During a vacancy in an archbishopric or diocesan bishopric the functions of an archbishop or a diocesan bishop under these rules shall be exercisable by the guardian of the spiritualities.[1]

(7) An archbishop or diocesan bishop or, during a vacancy, the guardian of the spiritualities may for any period of absence abroad or incapacity through illness appoint a commissary and delegate to him all or any of the functions of the archbishop or bishop under these rules, and, where during a vacancy, the guardian of the spiritualities is a corporation aggregate,[2] it shall appoint a commissary and delegate to him such functions as cannot appropriately be exercised by the corporation.

*Meaning of Minister, Parish and other words and phrases*

**44.** (1) In these rules:—

"actual communicant member" means a member who has

[1] See p. 1 *ante*.

[2] i.e. the dean and chapter of a vacant arch-see: see p. 1 *ante*.

received Communion according to the use of the Church of England or of another Church of the Anglican Communion or any overseas Church in communion with the Church of England at least three times during the twelve months preceding the date of his election or appointment;

"the Measure" means the Synodical Government Measure 1969;

"minister" means:—

(*a*) the incumbent of a parish;

(*b*) a curate licensed to the charge of a parish or a minister acting as priest-in-charge of a parish in respect of which rights of presentation are suspended; and

(*c*) a vicar in a team ministry to the extent that the duties of a minister are assigned to him by a scheme under the Pastoral Measure 1968 or his license [*sic*] from the bishop;

"parish" means:—

(*a*) an ecclesiastical parish; and

(*b*) a district which is constituted a "conventional district" for the cure of souls and has a separate curate licensed thereto.

"public worship" means public worship according to the rites and ceremonies of the Church of England.

(2) Any reference in these rules to the laity shall be construed as a reference to persons other than Clerks in Holy Orders, and the expression "lay" in these rules shall be construed accordingly.

(3) References in these rules to the cathedral church of the diocese shall include, in the case of the dioceses of London and Oxford, references to Westminster Abbey and St. George's Chapel, Windsor, respectively.

(4) If any question arises as to whether a Church is a Church of the Anglican Communion or an overseas Church in communion with the Church of England, it shall be conclusively determined for the purposes of these rules by the Archbishops of Canterbury and York.

(5) In these rules words importing residence include residence of a regular nature but do not include residence of a casual nature.

(6) Any reference herein to "these rules" shall be construed as including a reference to the Appendices hereto.

# APPENDIX I

## Section 1

Rule 1(2)

## APPLICATION FOR ENROLMENT ON CHURCH ELECTORAL ROLL

(Full Christian name and surname)

I ......................................................................................

(Full postal address)

of ......................................................................................

declare:—

(i) I am baptised.

(ii) I am a member of the Church of England.

or

I am a member of

, being a Church of the Anglican Communion or an overseas Church in communion with the Church of England.*

(iii) I am not a member of any other religious body which is not in communion with the Church of England.

(iv) I have attained the age of seventeen years.

(v) I am resident in the parish to which this application relates.

or

I am not resident in the parish and have habitually attended public worship in the parish in the last six months.*

(vi) My name is not on the church electoral roll of any other parish.

or

my name is not on the church electoral roll of any other parish except that of the parish of..................................................
from which roll I desire my name to be removed.

or

my name is not on the church electoral roll of any other parish except that of the parish of..................................................
The parochial church council of that parish has given its consent to my name being on the rolls of both parishes for so long as I retain the necessary qualifications.*

I hereby apply to have my name entered on the Church Electoral Roll of the parish of................................................................
in the diocese of................................................................

Signed ........................

Date ..............................

---

* Strike out whichever of the two or three possibilities is not applicable.

Section 2

Form 2(1)

## FORM OF NOTICE OF REVISION OF CHURCH ELECTORAL ROLL

Diocese of..............................................................................

Parish of ..............................................................................

Notice is hereby given that the Church Electoral Roll of the above parish will be revised by the Parochial Church Council,* beginning on

............the............day of........................... 19...... and ending

on.................., the.................day of.................. 19......

After such Revision, a copy of the Roll will forthwith be exhibited on, or near to, the principal door of the Parish Church for inspection.

Under the Church Representation Rules any persons are entitled to have their names entered on the roll, if they:—

(i) are baptised,

(ii) are members of the Church of England or another Church of the Anglican Communion or an overseas Church in communion with the Church of England, and are not members of any other religious body which is not in communion with the Church of England,

(iii) are seventeen or over,

(iv) are resident in the parish, or, not being resident in the parish, have habitually attended public worship in the parish during the six months before the date of application for enrolment, and

(v) have signed a form of application for enrolment.

Entry on the Rolls of two parishes at the same time is subject to special conditions. No person's name may be on the Rolls of more than two parishes at once.

Forms of application for enrolment can be obtained from the undersigned, and should be returned, if possible, in time for the Revision.

Any error discovered in the Roll should at once be reported to the undersigned.

Dated this** ....................... day of ....................... 19......

Electoral Roll Officer
Address .......................

---

\* NOTE—The Revision must be completed not less than 15 days or more than 28 days before the Annual Parochial Church Meeting.

\*\* Not less than 14 days notice must be given.

H

Section 3

Rule 2(4)

## FORM OF NOTICE OF PREPARATION OF NEW ROLL

Diocese of...........................................................................

Parish of ...........................................................................

Notice is hereby given that under the Church Representation Rules a new Church Electoral Roll is being prepared. All persons who wish to have their names entered on the new Roll, whether their names are entered on the present Roll or not, are requested to apply for enrolment if possible not later than..............................................................

...........................................................................................

The new roll will come into operation on....................................

...........................................................................................

Forms of application for enrolment can be obtained from the undersigned.

Under the Church Representation Rules any persons are entitled to have their names entered on the Roll, if they:—

(i) are baptised,
    are members of the Church of England or another Church of the Angican Communion or an overseas Church in communion therewith, and are not members of any other religious body which is not in communion with the Church of England.

(iii) are seventeen or over,

(iv) are resident in the parish, or, not being resident in the parish, have habitually attended public worship in the parish during the six months before the date of application for enrolment, and

(v) have signed a form of application for enrolment.

Entry on the Rolls of two parishes at the same time is subject to special conditions. No person's name may be on the Rolls of more than two parishes at once.

Any error discovered on the Roll should at once be reported to the undersigned.

Dated this ..................... day of ..........................
19......

Electoral Roll Officer

Address .................................

---

\* NOTE—The new roll must be completed not less than 15 days or more than 28 days before the Annual Parochial Church Meeting.

Section 4

Rule 6(1)

## NOTICE OF ANNUAL PAROCHIAL CHURCH MEETING

Parish of ..................................................................................

The Annual Parochial Church Meeting will be held in....................

....................................................................................................

on........................ day of ..................................... at ...............

For the election of Parochial representatives of the laity as follows:—

    To the Parochial Church Council....................representatives.

    * To the Deanery Synod................................representatives.

For the election of Sidesmen.

For the consideration of:—

(*a*) A copy or copies of the Roll;

(*b*) An Annual Report on the proceedings of the Council;

(*c*) An Annual Report on the financial affairs of the parish;

(*d*) The audited Accounts of the Council for the year ending on the 31st December immediately preceding the meeting;

(*e*) An audited Statement of the funds and property of the Council;

(*f*) A Report upon the fabric, goods and ornaments of the church or churches of the parish;

(*g*) A Report on the proceedings of the Deanery Synod;

and other matters of parochial or general Church interest.

All persons whose names are entered upon the Church Electoral Roll of the parish (and such persons only) are entitled to vote at the election of parochial representatives of the laity.

Such persons may object to the inclusion on or omission from the roll of any name but must do so before the commencement of elections.

Parochial representatives of the laity must be lay persons who have communicated at least three times in the year before the annual meeting in the Church of England or another Church of the Anglican Communion or an overseas Church in communion with the Church of England. For the parochial church council they must be at least seventeen and have their names on the electoral roll of the parish. For the deanery synod they must be of age to vote at a Parliamentary election and have their names on the roll of one of the parishes in the area in question.

Any person whose name is on the roll may be a sidesman.

Signed .............................. \*\*Minister of the parish.

---

* Include where applicable.

\*\* Or "Vice-Chairman of the Parochial Church Council" as the case may be (see rule 6(3) of the Church Representation Rules).

The remaining Sections of this Appendix relate only to diocesan synods and are here omitted.

# APPENDIX II

GENERAL PROVISIONS RELATING TO PAROCHIAL CHURCH
COUNCILS

**Rule 13
Officers of the
council.**

1.—(*a*) The minister of the parish shall be chairman of
the parochial church council (hereinafter referred to as
"the council").

(*b*) A lay member of the council shall be elected as vice-
chairman of the council.

(*c*) During the vacancy of the benefice and when the
chairman is incapacitated by absence or illness or any
other cause the vice-chairman of the council shall act as
chairman and have all the powers vested in the chairman.

(*d*) The council may appoint one of their number to act
as secretary of the council. If no member is appointed so
to act the council shall appoint some other fit person with
such remuneration (if any) as they shall think fit. The
secretary shall have charge of all documents relating to
the current business of the council except that, unless he is
the electoral roll officer, he shall not have charge of the
roll. He shall be responsible for keeping the minutes, shall
record all resolutions passed by the council and shall keep
the secretary of the diocesan synod and deanery synod
informed as to his name and address.

(*e*) The council may appoint one or more of their number to act as treasurer solely or jointly. Failing such
appointment, the office of treasurer shall be discharged
jointly by such of the churchwardens as are members of
the council, or, if there is only one such churchwarden, by
the churchwarden solely. No remuneration shall be paid
to any person in respect of his appointment as treasurer.

(*f*) The council shall appoint an electoral roll officer,
who may but need not be a member of the council and
may be the secretary, and if he is not a member may pay
to him such remuneration as it shall think fit. He shall
have charge of the roll.

(*g*) If auditors to the council are not appointed by the
annual meeting, or if auditors appointed by the annual
meeting are unable or unwilling to act, auditors shall be

appointed by the council. The remuneration (if any) of the auditors shall be paid by the council.

2. The council shall hold not less than four meetings in each year. Meetings shall be convened by the chairman and if not more than four meetings are held they shall be at quarterly intervals so far as possible. **Meetings of council.**

3. The chairman may at any time convene a meeting of the council. If he refuse or neglect to do so within seven days after a requisition for that purpose signed by not less than one-third of the members of the council has been presented to him those members may forthwith convene a meeting. **Power to call meetings.**

4.—(*a*) Except as provided in paragraph 8 of this Appendix, at least ten clear days before any meeting of the council notice thereof specifying the time and place of the intended meeting and signed by or on behalf of the chairman of the council or the persons convening the meeting shall be posted at or near the principal door of every church, or building licensed for public worship in the parish. **Notices relating to meetings.**

(*b*) Not less than seven days before the meeting a notice thereof specifying the time and place of the meeting signed by or on behalf of the secretary shall be sent to every member of the council. Such notice shall contain the agenda of the meeting including any motion or other business proposed by any member of the council of which notice has been received by the secretary.

5. Subject to the provisions of rule 18 the chair at a meeting of the council shall be taken:— **Chairman at meetings.**

(*a*) by the chairman of the council if he is present;

(*b*) if the chairman of the council is not present, or his office is vacant, by the vice-chairman of the council if he is present:

Provided that at any such meeting the chairman or the vice-chairman of the council shall, if he thinks it expedient to do so or the meeting so resolves, vacate the chair either generally or for the purposes of any business in which he has a personal interest or for any other particular business.

Should neither the chairman or vice-chairman be available to take the chair for any meeting or for any particular item on the agenda during a meeting then a chairman shall be chosen by those members present from among their number and the person so chosen shall preside for that meeting or for that particular item.

Quorum and agenda.

6. No business shall be transacted at any meeting of the council unless at least one-third of the members are present thereat and no business which is not specified in the agenda shall be transacted at any meeting except by the consent of three-quarters of the members present at the meeting.

Order of business.

7. The business of a meeting of the council shall be transacted in the order set forth in the agenda unless the council by resolution otherwise determine.

Short notice for emergency meetings.

8. In case of sudden emergency or other special circumstances requiring immediate action by the council a meeting may be convened by the chairman of the council at not less than three days' notice in writing to the members of the council but the quorum for the transaction of any business at such meetings shall be a majority of the then existing members of the council and no business shall be transacted at such meeting except as is specified in the notice convening the meeting.

Place of meetings.

9. The meeting of the council shall be held at such place as the council may direct or in the absence of such direction as the chairman may direct.

Vote of majority to decide.

10. The business of the Council shall be decided by a majority of the members present and voting thereon.

Casting vote.

11. In the case of an equal division of votes the chairman of the meeting shall have a second or casting vote.

Minutes.

12.—(*a*) The names of the members present at any meeting of the council shall be recorded in the minutes.

(*b*) If one-fifth of the members present and voting on any resolution so require, the minutes shall record the names of the members voting for and against that resolution.

(*c*) Any member of the council shall be entitled to require that the minutes shall contain a record of the manner in which his vote was cast on any resolution.

(*d*) Members of the council shall have access to the minutes of all meetings, but no other person other than the bishop or a person authorised by him in writing, or the archdeacon, shall have access to the minutes without the authority of the council.

13. Any meeting of the council may adjourn its proceedings to such time and place as may be determined at such meeting. **Adjournments.**

14.—(*a*) The council shall have a standing committee consisting of not less than five persons. The minister and such of the churchwardens as are members of the council shall be ex-officio members of the standing committee, and the council shall by resolution appoint at least two other members of the standing committee from among its own members and may remove any person so appointed. **Standing committee.**

(*b*) The standing committee shall have power to transact the business of the council between the meetings thereof subject to any directions given by the council.

15. The council may appoint other committees for the purpose of the various branches of church work in the parish and may include therein persons who are not members of the council. The minister shall be a member of all committees ex-officio. **Other committees.**

16. No proceedings of the council shall be invalidated by any vacancy in the membership of the council or by any defect in the qualification or election of any member thereof. **Validity of proceedings.**

17. Any question arising on the interpretation of this Appendix shall be referred to the bishop of the diocese and any decision given by him or by any person appointed by him on his behalf shall be final.[1] **Interpretation.**


## (3) THE PAROCHIAL CHURCH COUNCILS (POWERS) MEASURE 1956 (AS AMENDED) WITH NOTES

A MEASURE to consolidate with amendments certain enactments relating to parochial church councils and parochial charities.　　　　　　　　　　　　[5th July, 1956.]

---

[1] It has recently been held that this provision does not oust the jurisdiction of the ordinary courts on a question of interpretation.

**Definitions.**

**1.** In this Measure—

'Council' means a parochial church council;

'Diocesan Authority' means the Diocesan Board of Finance or any existing or future body appointed by the Diocesan Conference to act as trustees of diocesan trust property;

'Minister' and 'Parish' have the meanings respectively assigned to them in the Rules for the Representation of the Laity;[1]

'Relevant date' means the first day of July, 1921.[2]

**General functions of council.**

**2.**[3] (1) It shall be the duty of the incumbent and the parochial church council to consult together on matters of general concern and importance to the parish.

(2) The functions of parochial church councils shall include—

(a) co-operation with the incumbent in promoting in the parish the whole mission of the Church, pastoral, evangelistic, social and ecumenical;

(b) the consideration and discussions of matters concerning the Church of England or any other matters of religious or public interest, but not the declaration of the doctrine of the Church on any question;

(c) making known and putting into effect any provision made by the diocesan synod or the deanery synod, but without prejudice to the powers of the council on any particular matter;

(d) giving advice to the diocesan synod and the deanery synod on any matter referred to the council;

---

[1] These Rules have been replaced by the Church Representation Rules (Synodical Government Measure 1969, Schedule 3). The relevant definitions are now contained in Rule 44 of the last-mentioned Rules (p. 102 *ante*).

[2] The date of the coming into force of the original Parochial Church Councils (Powers) Measure 1921, which this Measure has replaced.

[3] This section was substituted by the Synodical Government Measure 1969 for the original section 2, which read: 'It shall be the primary duty of the council in every parish to co-operate with the minister in the initiation, conduct and development of church work both within the parish and outside.' The new section, in accordance with the general scheme of synodical government, lays greater emphasis on the part to be played by the laity.

(*e*) raising such matters as the council consider appropriate with the diocesan synod or deanery synod.

(3) In the exercise of its functions the parochial church council shall take into consideration any expression of opinion by any parochial church meeting.

**3.** Every council shall be a body corporate by the name of the parochial church council of the parish for which it is appointed and shall have perpetual succession.[1] Any act of the council may be signified by an instrument executed pursuant to a resolution of the council and under the hands or if an instrument under seal is required under the hands and seals of the chairman presiding and two other members of the council present at the meeting at which such resolution is passed.

*Council to be a body corporate.*

**4.** (1) Subject to the provisions of any Act or Measure passed after the relevant date and to anything lawfully done under such provisions, the council of every parish shall have—

*Powers vested in council as successor to certain other bodies.*

(i) The like powers duties and liabilities as immediately before the relevant date, the vestry[2] of such parish had with respect to the affairs of the church except as regards the election of churchwardens and sidesmen[3] and as

---

[1] These words give the council a corporate existence independent of the personnel comprised in it. It is a separate entity recognised by law, and exists as such for all time.

[2] The vestry was a parochial body which included the incumbent or curate-in-charge, and the persons of both sexes who were rated for the relief of the poor in respect of the parish, whether resident therein or not, and the occupiers of hereditaments so rated. It originally had both civil and ecclesiastical functions, but it was deprived of practically all its civil functions by statute many years ago. Immediately before the coming into force of the Parochial Church Council (Powers) Measure 1921, its principal ecclesiastical functions were the election of churchwardens and the other matters specified (whether as included in or as excluded from the transfer of functions to the council) in this present paragraph (i).

[3] As to the modern law relating to the appointment of churchwardens, see Chapter VIII *ante*. As to the election of sidesmen by the annual parochial church meeting, see p. 90 *ante*.

regards the administration of ecclesiastical charities[1] but including the power of presentation to the benefice of such parish if the right to present thereto was vested in or in trust for the parishioners and the power of making any voluntary church rate.[2]

(ii) The like powers duties and liabilities as, immediately before the relevant date, the churchwardens of such parish had with respect to—

(a) The financial affairs of the Church including the collection and administration of all moneys raised for church purposes and the keeping of accounts in relation to such affairs and moneys;[3]

(b) The care maintenance preservation and insurance

---

[1] Broadly speaking, this expression covers every charity for the religious purposes of any church or denomination. The administration of any such charity which was originally vested in the vestry remains so vested.

[2] The right to enforce or compel the payment of a church rate in any ecclesiastical or other court was taken away by the Compulsory Church Rates Abolition Act 1868; but the same Act expressly reserved the power for vestries, in both ancient and modern parishes and districts, to make and assess a church rate, on the footing that payment by the person on whom it is assessed is voluntary. A 'church rate' is defined for this purpose as a rate for ecclesiastical purposes, i.e. for the 'building, rebuilding, enlargement and repair of any church or chapel, and any purpose to which by common or ecclesiastical law a church rate is applicable, or any of such purposes.'

The Act did not affect the recovery of church rates specially imposed by any private or local Act of Parliament, where the power to levy the rate was conferred for valuable consideration (such as the extinguishment of tithes or customary payments) of a nature specified in the Act. Such rates are still enforceable.

In practice, the power conferred by the Act to make a voluntary church rate was never of much value, and its use at the present day is extremely rare. But for what it is worth it is now vested in the parochial church council. When it is proposed to exercise it, it would appear that it is the duty of the churchwardens to prepare an estimate of the sum required and to lay it before the council, in the same way as they formerly prepared such an estimate and laid it before the vestry. After the churchwardens have done this they are relieved of responsibility.

[3] As to money collected in church, see section 7(iv) *post*, and note thereto.

of the fabric of the church and the goods and ornaments thereof[1];

(*c*) The care and maintenance of the churchyard (open or closed), and the power of giving a certificate under the provisions of section eighteen of the Burial Act, 1855, with the like powers as immediately before the relevant date were possessed by the churchwardens to recover the cost of maintaining a closed churchyard;[2]

Provided that nothing herein contained shall affect the property[3] of the churchwardens in the goods and ornaments of the church or their powers duties and liabilities with respect to visitations.[4]

(iii) The like powers duties and liabilities as, immediately before the relevant date, were possessed by the church trustees[5] (if any) for the parish appointed under the Compulsory Church Rate Abolition Act, 1868.

---

[1] There is no *duty* to insure except a moral one. The general duty of repair now extends to the chancel when the incumbent is rector, by virtue of section 52 of the Ecclesiastical Dilapidations Measure 1923. A *lay* rector remains personally liable for the repair of the chancel, except in those cases (probably the majority) where the liability has been voluntarily compounded under the provisions of the Act of 1923, or has been extinguished under the terms of the Tithe Act 1936.

[2] A churchyard may be 'closed', i.e. discontinued for burials, by an Order in Council made under the Burial Acts. Under section 18 of the Burial Act 1855, the duty of maintaining a churchyard so closed in decent order, and its walls and fences repaired, was cast upon the churchwardens. The expenses incurred were, however, recoverable by them out of the general rate upon their certifying the amount. When once such a certificate had been given, the powers, duties and liabilities of the churchwardens in regard to the repair and maintenance of the closed churchyard passed automatically to the appropriate local authority (being the borough or urban district or parish council as the case might be).

The law is still as just stated, save that under the present provision the parochial church council is substituted for the churchwardens.

[3] Property in this context means 'legal ownership'.

[4] Churchwardens thus retain their powers of making 'presentments', their duties in respect of answering the questions contained in the visitation articles and of attending visitations for the purpose of being admitted to office, and (presumably) their liability to pay the visitation fees.

[5] 'Church trustees' originated from section 9 of the Compulsory

(2) All enactments in any Act whether general or local or personal[1] relating to any powers duties or liabilities transferred to the council from the vestry churchwardens or church trustees as the case may be shall subject to the provisions of this Measure and so far as circumstances admit be construed as if any reference therein to the vestry or the churchwardens or church trustees referred to the council to which such powers duties or liabilities have been transferred and the said enactments shall be construed with such modifications as may be necessary for carrying this Measure into effect.

(3) Where any property is applicable to purposes connected with any such powers duties or liabilities as aforesaid, any deed or instrument which could be or could have been made or executed in relation to such property by a vestry, or by churchwardens or church trustees, may be made or executed by the council of the parish concerned.

(4) This Measure shall not affect any enactment in any

---

Church Rates Abolition Act 1868, which gave power to appoint a body of trustees in any parish for the purpose of accepting, by bequest or otherwise, and of holding, any contributions which might be given to them for ecclesiastical purposes in the parish. Their powers included the investment of funds in their hands, accumulation of the income, and (subject to any conditions attached by the donors) power to pay over such funds to the churchwardens for expenditure on the ecclesiastical purposes of the parish. The trustees under the section were the incumbent and two householders or owners or occupiers of land in the parish, one chosen by the patron and one by the bishop.

The result of this present provision is that all the powers and functions of church trustees have passed to the parochial church council, and the church trustees and the power to appoint them have been swept away. Presumably, in the light of the fact that all the functions of the churchwardens in relation to the financial affairs of the Church have, under section 4(1)(ii)(c) *ante*, been transferred to the parochial church council, the council should itself apply any funds required for the ecclesiastical purposes of the parish, instead of paying them over to the churchwardens as section 9 of the Act of 1868 originally required.

[1] An Act affecting the whole or a considerable part of the realm is said to be a general Act, because it is of general application. A local Act is one which applies to a particular locality, and a personal (sometimes called 'private') Act is one which affects only a particular person or class of persons.

private or local Act of Parliament under the authority of which church rates[1] may be made or levied in lieu of or in consideration of the extinguishment or of the appropriation to any other purpose of any tithes customary payments or other property or charge upon property which tithes payments property or charge previously to the passing of such Act had been appropriated by law to ecclesiastical purposes or in consideration of the abolition of tithes in any place or upon any contract made or for good or valuable consideration given and every such enactment shall continue in force in the same manner as if this Measure had not been passed.

For the purposes of this subsection 'ecclesiastical purposes' shall mean the building rebuilding enlargement and repair of any church or chapel and any purpose to which by common[2] or ecclesiastical law a church rate is applicable or any of such purposes.

**5.** (1) Subject to the provisions of this Measure, the council of every parish shall have power to acquire (whether by way of gift or otherwise) any property real or personal[3] **Holding of property for ecclesiastical purposes: educational schemes.**

(*a*) For any ecclesiastical purpose affecting the parish or any part thereof;

(*b*) For any purpose in connection with schemes (hereinafter called 'educational schemes') for providing facilities

---

[1] The reference here is to those church rates, imposed by private or local Acts, which were excepted from abolition by the Compulsory Church Rates Abolition Act 1868; see section 4(1)(i) *ante* and the notes thereto. Since the Measure does not affect the enactments imposing such rates, they are still to be levied by the authority originally empowered to do so, and not by the parochial church council.

[2] The common law is that part of the law of England, other than statute, which has existed continually since before legal memory. 'Ecclesiastical law' is a vague phrase, but it would certainly include the canon law which, so far as it binds the laity, has long ago become incorporated in the common law or in Acts of Parliament.

[3] All property is in law divided into real and personal property. The distinction is technical, but it may be taken that the two classes together embrace every kind of property.

for the spiritual moral and physical training of persons residing in or near the parish.

(2) Subject to the provisions of this Measure and of the general law and to the provisions of any trusts affecting any such property, the council shall have power to manage, administer and dispose of any property acquired under this section.

(3) A council shall have power, in connection with any educational scheme, to constitute or participate in the constitution of a body of managers or trustees or a managing committee consisting either wholly or partly of persons appointed by the council, and may confer on any such body or committee such functions in regard to the implementation of the scheme, and such functions relating to property held for the purposes of the scheme, as the council thinks expedient.

(4) The powers of a council with respect to educational schemes shall be exercised subject to and in accordance with the terms of any undertaking which may have been given by the council to the Minister of Education or to any local authority in connection with any financial or other assistance given by the Minister or the authority in relation to the scheme.

(5) A council shall not exercise any of its powers in relation to educational schemes without the consent of the diocesan education committee of the diocese, and any such consent may be given upon such terms and conditions as the committee considers appropriate in all the circumstances of the case.

In this subsection the expression 'diocesan education committee' includes any body of persons whether incorporated or not for the time being having the functions of such a committee by virtue of the Diocesan Education Committees Measure, 1955, and any orders made thereunder.

**Supplementary provisions relating to certain property.**

**6.** (1) After the commencement of this Measure,[1] a council shall not acquire any interest in land (other than

---

[1] i.e. the 2nd January, 1957: see section 10(2) *post*.

a short lease as hereinafter defined) or in any personal property to be held on permanent trusts, without the consent of the diocesan authority.[1]

(2) Where, at or after the commencement of this Measure, a council holds or acquires an interest in land (other than a short lease as hereinafter defined) or any interest in personal property to be held on permanent trusts, such interest shall be vested in the diocesan authority subject to all trusts, debts and liabilities affecting the same, and all persons concerned shall make or concur in making such transfers (if any) as are requisite for giving effect to the provisions of this subsection.

(3) Where any property is vested in the diocesan authority pursuant to subsection (2) of this section, the council shall not sell, lease, let, exchange, charge or take any legal proceedings with respect to the property without the consent of the authority; but save as aforesaid, nothing in this section shall affect the powers of the council in relation to the management, administration or disposition of any such property.

(4) Where any property is vested in the diocesan authority pursuant to subsection (2) of this section, the council shall keep the authority indemnified in respect of:

(*a*) all liabilities subject to which the property is vested in the authority or which may thereafter be incident to the property;

(*b*) all rates, taxes, insurance premiums and other outgoings of whatever nature which may from time to time be payable in respect of the property;

(*c*) all costs, charges and expenses incurred by the authority in relation to the acquisition or insurance of the property or as trustee thereof;

(*d*) all costs, proceedings, claims and demands in respect of any of the matters hereinbefore mentioned.

(5) The consents required by subsection (3) of this section are additional to any other consents required by law, either from the Charity Commissioners or the Minister of Education or otherwise.

---

[1] See section 1, p. 112 *ante.*

(6) In this section the expression 'short lease' means a lease for a term not exceeding one year, and includes any tenancy from week to week, from month to month, from quarter to quarter, or from year to year.

(7) Any question as to whether personal property is to be held on permanent trusts shall be determined for the purposes of this section by a person appointed by the bishop.

**Miscellaneous powers of Council.**

7. The council of every parish shall have the following powers in addition to any powers conferred by the Constitution or otherwise by this Measure:—

(i) Power to frame an annual budget of moneys required for the maintenance of the work of the Church in the parish and otherwise and to take such steps as they think necessary for the raising collecting and allocating of such moneys;

(ii) Power to make levy and collect a voluntary church rate for any purpose connected with the affairs of the church including the administrative expenses of the council and the costs of any legal proceedings;[1]

(iii) Power jointly with the minister to appoint and dismiss the parish clerk and sexton or any persons performing or assisting to perform the duties of parish clerk or sexton and to determine their salaries and the conditions of the tenure of their offices or of their employment but subject to the rights of any persons holding the said offices at the appointed day;[2]

(iv) Power jointly with the minister to determine the objects to which all moneys to be given or collected in church shall be allocated subject to the directions contained

---

[1] This is a new power to levy a voluntary church rate, additional to the power to levy such a rate which has been transferred from the vestry to the council; see section 4(1)(i) *ante*, and the notes thereto. The purposes for which a rate may be levied under the new power would appear to be somewhat wider than those for which a rate may be levied under the transferred power.

[2] See Chapter X *ante*. The expression 'appointed day' presumably means the 1st July 1921, which is the 'relevant date' as defined by section 1 of the Measure.

in the Book of Common Prayer as to the disposal of money given at the offertory;[1]

(v) Power to make representations to the bishop with regard to any matter affecting the welfare of the church in the parish.[2]

**8.** (1) Every council shall furnish to the annual church meeting the audited accounts of the council for the year ending on the 31st December immediately preceding the meeting and an audited statement of the funds and property, if any, remaining in the hands of the council at that date. **Accounts of the Council.**

(2) At least seven days before the annual parochial church meeting, the council shall cause a copy of the said audited accounts and a copy of the said statement to be affixed at or near the principal door of the parish church as required by paragraph (2) of Rule 8 of the Rules for the Representation of the Laity.[3]

(3) The accounts and statement shall be submitted to the meeting for approval, and, if approved, they shall be signed by the chairman of the meeting who shall then deliver them to the council for publication, and the council shall forthwith cause them to be published in the manner provided by paragraph (3) of Rule 8 of the Rules for the Representation of the Laity.[4]

(4) The accounts of all trusts administered by the council shall be laid before the Diocesan Authority[5] annually.

---

[1] The position as to church collections may be summarised as follows: the churchwardens (jointly with the incumbent) are solely responsible for the Communion alms; the council (jointly with the incumbent) is responsible for the money collected at other services. There should therefore be two accounts, a churchwarden's account and a council account. The only charge to which the former is liable is the visitation fee.

[2] This places the council in the same position as an individual parishioner who *may* make such representations. In certain circumstances (see p. 70 *ante*) the churchwardens are under a duty to do so.

[3] Now Rule 8(2) of the Church Representation Rules: see p. 89 *ante*.

[4] Now Rule 8(3) of the Church Representation Rules: see p. 89 *ante*.

[5] See section 1, p. 112 *ante*.

I

**Powers of bishop.**

**9.** (1) The bishop may subject to the provisions of this Measure and the Constitution[1] make rules for carrying this Measure into effect within the diocese.

(2) If any act required by this Measure to be done by any person is not done within such time as the bishop may consider reasonable it may be done by or under the authority of the bishop.

(3) In the event of a council and a minister being unable to agree as to any matter in which their agreement or joint action is required under the provisions of this Measure, such matter shall be dealt with or determined in such manner as the bishop may direct.

(4) During a vacancy in a diocesan see the powers conferred upon the bishop by this section may be exercised by the guardian of the spiritualities.[2]

**Short title, commencement, extent and repeals.**

**10.** (1) This Measure may be cited as the Parochial Church Councils (Powers) Measure, 1956.

(2) This Measure shall come into operation on the second day of January, 1957.

(3) This Measure shall extend to the whole of the Provinces of Canterbury and York except the Channel Islands and the Isle of Man:

Provided that, if an Act of Tynwald so provides, this Measure shall extend to the Isle of Man subject to such modifications, if any, as may be specified in such Act of Tynwald.

(4) The Parochial Church Councils (Powers) Measure, 1921, and the Parochial Church Councils (Powers) (Amendment) Measure, 1949, are hereby repealed.

---

[1] The 'Constitution' means the Constitution of the Church Assembly (now the General Synod) appended to the Church of England Assembly (Powers) Act 1919.

[2] i.e. the archbishop of the province: see p. 1 *ante.*

## (4) PROVISIONS OF PASTORAL MEASURE 1968 AS TO CHURCH MEETINGS AND COUNCILS IN CERTAIN CASES[1]

### SCHEDULE 3

**3.** (1) Where a pastoral scheme establishes a team ministry, the scheme, or the bishop's licence of any vicar in the team ministry, may assign to any such vicar the duties or a share in the duties of the chairmanship of the annual parochial church meeting and the parochial church council of the parish or any of the parishes in the area of the benefice for which the team ministry is established, and other duties of the minister of the parish under the Rules contained in the Schedule to the Representation of the Laity Measure 1956,[2] or a share in such other duties, and the said Rules shall have effect accordingly:

Provided that, if the said duties of chairmanship are to be shared, the arrangements shall be such that the chairman on any occasion is determined in advance so that, in his absence, the vice-chairman of the parochial church council[3] shall take the chair in accordance with the said Rules.

(2) Where a pastoral scheme establishes a team ministry, the scheme may provide or authorise the bishop by instrument under his hand with the concurrence of the rector to provide—

(*a*) for the election by the annual parochial church meeting of the parish or any of the parishes in the area of the benefice for which the team ministry is established, of a district church council for any district in the parish in which a church or place of worship is situated, and of deputy churchwardens for the church or place of worship;

(*b*) for assigning to the district church council and deputy churchwardens such of the functions of the parochial church council and the churchwardens of the parish, being functions relating to the said church or place of worship or district,

---

[1] The provisions in question are those contained in Schedule 3, paragraph 3 (relating to team and group ministries), paragraph 12 (relating to new parishes), and paragraph 13 (relating to united benefices and benefices held in plurality). The text of all three paragraphs is here set out.

[2] See now the Church Representation Rules p. 80 *ante*.

[3] The vice-chairman is always a layman: Church Representation Rules, Appendix II, paragraph 1(b) (p. 108 *ante*).

but not including their functions as interested parties under Part I of this Measure,[1] as may be specified by the scheme or determined thereunder;

(c) for a vicar in the team ministry to be the chairman of the district church council, and for the constitution, meetings and procedure of the council.

In this sub-paragraph "place of worship" means a building or part of a building licensed for public worship according to the rites and ceremonies of the Church of England.

(3) All vicars in a team ministry shall be entitled to attend the parochial church meetings, and shall be ex officio members of the parochial church council, of the parish or each of the parishes in the area of the benefice for which the team ministry is established, and the rector and all the vicars shall have a right to attend the meetings of any district church council elected for any district in a parish.

(4) Where a pastoral scheme establishes a group ministry or establishes a team ministry for an area comprising more than one parish, the scheme may provide or authorise the bishop by instrument under his hand with the concurrence of all the members of the group or team ministry to provide—

(a) for establishing a group council, comprising all the said members and such number of lay representatives of each of the parochial church councils in the area for which the group or team ministry is established as may be specified in the scheme, for the purpose of consulting together on matters of common concern;

(b) for the election of the lay representatives by the said councils;

(c) for the chairmanship, meetings and proceedings of the group council.

(5) All the incumbents in a group ministry shall be entitled to attend the parochial church meetings and the meetings of the parochial church councils of all the parishes in the area for which the group ministry is established.

**12.** (1) The incumbent of a new parish created by a pastoral scheme shall as soon as possible, according to the provisions of

[1] 'Interested parties' are parties who have special rights to be informed and consulted in respect of any proposed new pastoral scheme or order, and they include the parochial church councils of any parishes liable to be affected by the proposed scheme or order.

the Rules contained in the Schedule to the Representation of the Laity Measure 1956,[1] take all necessary steps—

(*a*) to form a church electoral roll, and

(*b*) to convene a special parochial church meeting.

(2) A special meeting so convened shall, in addition to any other business, elect representatives of the laity to the parochial church council, to the ruridecanal conference (if any) and the diocesan conference[2] if such representatives are required to be elected at annual meetings of that new parish.

(3) A special meeting so convened and held in the month of November or the month of December may, if the meeting so resolves, be for all purposes under the said Rules the annual parochial church meeting for the succeeding year, and a special meeting so convened shall in any event be for all such purposes the annual parochial church meeting for the year in which it is so convened and held.

(4) Without prejudice to any general rule of law relating to parochial church councils, the powers, duties and liabilities set out in section 4(1)(ii) of the Parochial Church Councils (Powers) Measure 1956[3] shall continue to apply to any church which was formerly a parish church and becomes a chapel of ease as the result of a pastoral scheme or order, and to the churchyard of any such church, except so far as the scheme or order otherwise provides.

**13.** Where there are two or more parishes within the area of a single benefice or two or more benefices are held in plurality, a pastoral scheme or order may provide for constituting a joint parochial church council for all or some of the parishes of the benefice or benefices and for empowering that council to exercise such of the powers of the parochial church councils of the several parishes concerned as may be determined by or in accordance with the scheme or order, and the scheme or order may apply in relation to the joint parochial church council, with such modifica-

[1] See now the Church Representation Rules, p. 80 *ante*.

[2] The deanery synod should now be substituted for the ruri-decanal conference: Synodical Government Measure 1969, section 5(2). So far as the diocesan conference is concerned, this provision has altogether ceased to have effect, since the diocesan conference is now extinct, and the lay representatives on the diocesan synod which has taken its place are not elected by parochial church meetings.

[3] See p. 114 *ante*.

tions as may be specified, the provisions of any Measure relating to parochial church councils, and may make provision for vesting in the joint parochial church council any property, rights and liabilities of the parochial church councils of the several parishes concerned.

# CHAPTER XII

# CONDUCT OF MEETINGS

The preceding chapters of this book have been designed with a view to placing the rights and duties of the laity in the parishes in their proper and larger context of the Church of which they are members, and to affording guidance to them in the interpretation of their position, especially in the light of modern legislation.

In this concluding chapter some attempt is made to assist them in the normal conduct of their business, particularly in parochial church councils.

The chairman of the council is normally the incumbent of the parish, and in his absence his place is taken by a lay vice-chairman elected by the council. The incumbent is a member of all committees of the council, but not necessarily the chairman of a committee.

The incumbent is primarily responsible for convening parochial church meetings and the parochial church council. In particular, he is under a legal duty to convene the annual parochial church meeting not later than the 30th April in every year, and at least four meetings of the parochial church council during the year. The provisions of the Church Representation Rules as to the notices of meetings[1] which must be given should be strictly observed; otherwise there is a risk of the proceedings at meetings being invalidated. The incumbent should instruct the secretary as to the form of agenda which is to be sent to the members.

Before the meeting of a parochial church council, the chairman should already have perused the draft minutes of the last meeting, the reading of which should be the first item of the agenda after prayers have been said. They should be compiled by the secretary from notes taken at the time, and should, before the meeting, have been submitted to the incumbent for his comments. In their

[1] See pp. 88, 109 *ante*.

127

final draft form they should be written in the minute book. It is important to remember that the minutes are intended to be a record of business transacted. It is unnecessary and sometimes inconvenient to give a detailed account of a discussion. The minutes should state, for example, that Mr. A. proposed, and Mr. B. seconded, a resolution (which should be set out in full). If an amendment is proposed and seconded, it should be similarly recorded. The minutes may state the name of any person who spoke in a debate, but this is not necessary. But it should be recorded, e.g., that a resolution or an amendment was carried (or defeated) and the number of votes given on either side in a division should always be stated. It is expressly provided by the Rules that if one-fifth of the members of a parochial church council present and voting on a resolution so require, the minutes should record the names of those voting for and against the resolution; also that any member is entitled to require the manner in which his vote was cast to be recorded.[1]

The names of those present at a meeting should always be recorded.

When the minutes have been read, the chairman should ask if they are a correct record. This is not an invitation to discuss the merits of what is recorded, but merely to obtain agreement that the record is correct. If exception is taken as to the accuracy of the record, that question may be debated and the council may vote either to accept the record or to amend it.

The chairman should then ask the council for authority to sign the minutes as read, or as amended, and when he has done so, they become the authentic account of the transactions recorded therein, and are receivable in evidence in any court of justice, if produced to that court by the chairman or secretary.

At this stage it is customary to deal with any business arising out of the minutes, other than business which forms a separate item on the agenda. After this has been disposed of, any correspondence received by the secretary (including apologies for non-attendance) should be read and the instructions of the council taken thereon.

Then the other items on the agenda are taken, one by one, and the decision of the council upon each of them arrived at. Voting is by a show of hands, and a resolution is decided by a simple

[1] See p. 110 *ante.*

majority of those present and voting, the chairman having a second or casting vote.

It is customary to include at the end of an agenda paper an item called 'Other Business'. It is within the competence of the council to deal with a matter not specifically mentioned on the agenda paper but the Rules require that three-quarters of the members present at the meeting must consent; and even if such consent is forthcoming, the chairman might reasonably, when the matter is important, rule that it is to be adjourned to a future meeting.

It is open to any member, at any stage in the proceedings, to raise a point of order. In doing so he must confine his remarks to the point of order; he should not be allowed to discuss the merits of the matter under debate. Thus it is in order to submit to the chairman that the matter is not one which it is within the competence of the meeting to discuss, but it is not in order to raise *in this way* the question of the expediency of such a discussion.

The decision whether the question is or is not a point of order rests with the chairman and he must decide it. When he has given his decision it must be accepted by the meeting.

Any member may address the council, but unless he is given leave he should not normally speak more than once in relation to the particular matter under discussion. But he should always be allowed to make an explanation or correction of what he has previously said, should he feel that this is desirable in the light of what is said by a member speaking subsequently to him. The chairman may not properly refuse to hear a member, but he has the right to decide on the order in which members may speak, and he may in a proper case stop any member who in his opinion is speaking irrelevantly to the matter under discussion.

If a point of order is raised, the chairman must first make up his mind that it really is a point of order. If he considers that it is, he must decide the point of order at once, i.e. before the general discussion is resumed.

# INDEX

Actual communicant member, *102*
Alms, *67, 68, 121*
Ancient parish, *30, 31*
Appeals, in relation to elections, *97, 98*
Archbishop:
  consecrates bishops, *1*
  court of, *23*
  guardian of spiritualities, *1*
  president of Convocation, *1*
Archdeacon, *3, 4*
  certificate of, *29*
  induction by, *41*
  visitation by, *3, 59*
Assistant Curate:
  guild church, of, *39*
  licence of, *2, 47, 48*
  oath by, *48*
  resignation of, *48*
  stipend of, *48*
Auditor, *90, 108, 109*

Benefice:
  avoidance of, *46*
  exchange of, *46*
  meaning of, *35*
  union of, *35*
  vacancy of, *68, 69, 79*
Benefices Act, *41, 51*
Benefices Act 1898 (Amendment) Measure, *52, 53*
Benefices (Exercise of Rights of Presentation) Measure, *53, 54*
Benefices (Purchase of Rights of Presentation) Measure, *54*
Benefices (Transfer of Rights of Presentation) Measure, *53*
Bishop:
  Church Representation Rules, powers under, *101, 102*
  churchwardens as officers of, *69, 70*
  consecration of, *1*

court of, *22*
institution by, *2, 41*
jurisdiction of, *2*
oath of, *2*
visitation by, *59*
Brawling, *66*

Canons:
  by Convocations, *5, 6*
  by General Synod, *7, 11*
Cession, *46*
Chancel, repairs of, *115*
Chancellor, *22*
  faculty jurisdiction of, *27, 28, 29*
Chapel-of-ease, *34*
  wardens of, *64, 65*
Chapelwardens, *64, 65*
Church:
  chapel-of-ease, *34*
  churchwardens' functions as to, *65, 66*
  pastoral scheme, affected by, *33, 34*
  redundant, *34*
Church Assembly, *5, 6*
Church of England Assembly (Powers) Act, *5, 6*
Church rate, *114, 117*
Church Representation Rules, *80*
Church trustees, *115, 116*
Churchwardens:
  actions by and against, *70*
  admission of, *58, 59*
  allocation of seats by, *66, 67*
  alms, duties as to, *67, 68*
  appointment of, *55, 56, 57*
  bishops' officers, *69, 70*
  casual vacancy, *57*
  church and churchyard, functions as to, *65, 66*
  collections, duties as to, *67, 68*
  custom as to appointing, *61*
  deputy, *64, 65, 95, 123*

131